Times and Seasons
Volume 1, Numbers 1-3

By
Ebenezer Robinson & Don Carlos Smith

Copyright © 2021 Lamp of Trismegistus. All rights reserved. No part of this publication may be reproduced or transmitted in any form or by any means, electronic or mechanical, including photocopying, recording, or by any information storage and retrieval system, without permission in writing from Lamp of Trismegistus. Reviewers may quote brief passages.

ISBN: 978-1-63118-555-7

Mormon History Series

Other Books in this Series and Related Titles

Pearl of Great Price by Joseph Smith (978-1-63118-539-7)

The Angel of the Prairies or A Dream of the Future: Mormon History Series By Elder Parley Parker Pratt (978-1-63118-541-0)

A Manuscript on Far West by Reed Peck (978-1-63118-544-1)

The Story of Mormonism by James E Talmage (978-1-63118-543-4)

Interesting Account of Several Remarkable Visions: Mormon History Series By Orson Pratt (978-1-63118-553-3)

An Address to All Believers in Christ Elder David Whitmer (978-1-63118-545-8)

The Philosophy of Mormonism by James E Talmage (978-1-63118-542-7)

The Book of Abraham: Mormon History by George Reynolds (978-1-63118-540-3)

The Testament of Abraham by Abraham (978-1-63118-441-3)

Private Diary of Joseph Smith 1832-1834 (978-1-63118-546-5)

The Book of John Whitmer by John Whitmer (978-1-63118-554-0)

The Evening and Morning Star Volume 1, Numbers 1 & 2 (978-1-63118-547-2)

The Evening and Morning Star Volume 1, Numbers 3 & 4 (978-1-63118-548-9)

The Evening and Morning Star Volume 1, Numbers 7 & 8 (978-1-63118-550-2)

The Evening and Morning Star Volume 1, Numbers 9 & 10 (978-1-63118-551-9)

The Testament of Moses by Moses (978-1-63118-440-6)

The Secrets of Enoch by Enoch (978-1-63118-449-9)

The Book of the Watchers by Enoch (978-1-63118-416-1)

Book of Dreams by Enoch (978-1-63118-437-6)

The Book of Astronomical Secrets by Enoch (978-1-63118-443-7)

Audio Versions are also available on Audible, Amazon and Apple

Other Books in this Series and Related Titles

The Hidden Mysteries of Christianity by Annie Besant (978–1–63118–534–2)

Rosicrucian Rules, Secret Signs, Codes and Symbols by various (978-1-63118-488-8)

History and Teachings of the Rosicrucians by W W Westcott &c (978-1-63118-487-1)

Freemasonry and the Egyptian Mysteries by C. W. Leadbeater (978-1-63118-456-7)

American Indian Freemasonry by A C Parker (978-1-63118-460-4)

The Psalms of Solomon by King Solomon (978-1-63118-439-0)

The Historic, Mythic and Mystic Christ by Annie Besant (978–1–63118–533–5)

Masonic and Rosicrucian History by M P Hall & H Voorhis (978-1-63118-486-4)

Some Deeper Aspects of Masonic Symbolism by A E Waite (978-1-63118-461-1)

Masonic Symbolism of King Solomon's Temple by A Mackey &c (978-1-63118-442-0)

The Old Past Master by Carl H Claudy (978-1-63118-464-2)

The Book of Parables by Enoch (978-1-63118-429-1)

The Mysteries of Freemasonry & the Druids by various (978-1-63118-444-4)

Masonic Symbolism of the Apron & the Altar by various (978-1-63118-428-4)

The Book of Wisdom of Solomon by King Solomon (978-1-63118-502-1)

Masonic Symbolism of Easter and the Christ in Masonry (978-1-63118-434-5)

The Odes of Solomon by King Solomon (978-1-63118-503-8)

Ancient Mysteries and Secret Societies by M P Hall (978-1-63118-410-9)

The Golden Verses of Pythagoras: Five Translations (978-1-63118-479-6)

Freemasonry & Catholicism by Max Heindel (978-1-63118-508-3)

A Few Masonic Sermons by A. C. Ward &c (978-1-63118-435-2)

Audio versions are also available on Audible, Amazon and Apple

Table of Contents

Times and Seasons

Volume 1

Number 1…7

Number 2…40

Number 3…74

TIMES AND SEASONS

"TRUTH WILL PREVAIL"

Vol. 1. Whole No.1.] COMMERCE, ILLINOIS, NOVEMBER 1839 [Whole No. 1

ADDRESS.

As this No. commences the Times and Seasons, it is but proper that we should lay before its readers, the course we intend to pursue, with regard to the editorial department of the same.

We wish to make it a source of light and instruction to all those who may peruse its columns, by laying before them, in plainness, the great plan of salvation which was devised in heaven from before the foundation of the world, as made known to the saints of God, in former, as well as latter days; and is, like its Author, the same in all ages, and changeth not.

In order for this, we may at times, dwell at considerable length, upon the fullness of the everlasting gospel of Jesus Christ, as laid down in the revealed word of God; the necessity of embracing it with full purpose of heart, and living by all its precepts; remembering the words of our Savior, "he that will be my disciple let him take up his cross and follow me."

We shall treat freely upon the gathering of Israel, which is to take place in these last days-of the dispensation of the fullness of times, when the fullness of the Gentiles is to come in, and the outcasts of Jacob be brought back to dwell upon the lands of their inheritance, preparatory to that great day of rest, which is soon to usher in, when Christ will reign with his saints upon earth, a thousand years, according to the testimony of all the holy prophets since the world began.

We shall also endeavor to give a detailed history of the persecution and suffering, which the members of the church of Jesus Christ of Latter Day Saints, has had to endure in Missouri, and elsewhere, for their religion. A mere synopsis of which, would swell this address to volumes; therefore we are compelled to let it pass for the present, by touching upon a few of its most prominent features.

In Jackson county, Missouri, in the year 1833, several were murdered-one whipped to death-a number shot-others whipped until they were literally cut to pieces, then left to die; but God, through his kindness, spared their lives- others tarred and feathered- between two and three hundred men had their houses plundered, and then burned to ashes, and they, with their wives and little ones, driven into the forests to perish.

Again, in 1836 they were informed by the citizens of Clay county Mo. (where they settled after being driven from Jackson,) that they could dwell there no longer; consequently they were compelled to seek a location elsewhere; notwithstanding the greater part of them had purchased the land upon which they lived, with their own money, with the expectation of securing to themselves and families, permanent abiding places, where they could dwell in peace: but in this they were mistaken, for in the latter part of this same year, they were obliged to move out of the country, when they went to a back prairie country, where the other citizens assured them they might dwell in safety.

Here they commenced their labors with renewed courage, firmly believing they were preparing peaceful homes, where they could spend the remainder of there days in the sweet enjoyment of that liberty which was so dearly bought by the blood of their venerable Fathers, but which had been so cruelly wrested from them, by the hands of their oppressors, in both Jackson and Clay counties. But here again they were sadly disappointed, for no sooner had they built comfortable dwelling places, and opened beautiful and extensive farms, which their untiring industry and perseverance soon accomplished, than their neighbors in the adjoining counties began to envy them, and look upon them with a jealous eye; so that in the year 1838, mobs again began to harrass and disturb them, by stealing their cattle and hogs, burning their houses. and shooting at their men; when they petitioned the Governor for protection, which he utterly refused. They then saw there was no other way but to stand in their own defence; which they prepared to do with all possible diligence. This was no sooner made known to the Governor, than he ordered out the militia, (report says THIRTY THOUSAND) about twelve thousand of which, were on the march and issued his Edict, Maximim [Maximum] like, to have the saints EXTERMINATED, or EXPELLED from the State forthwith. Accordingly, many were murdered, or rather martyred!-about 60 thrust into prison-several hundred families driven from their homes, in the short space of ten days, in the midst of a very remarkable snow storm in the month of November-their property plundered -- and the whole church, comprising about twelve thousand souls, expelled from the State!!

Thus you see, gentle reader, a minute history of all those transactions mentioned above, will be a subject of no small moment; when we consider that they have all been performed in the midst of this boasted land of Liberty; whose whole fabric, rests upon this one pivot, liberty of conscience.

Deprive her citizens of this heavenly boon, which is so freely granted to all, by the Author of our existance [existence], and all her hopes of future prosperity are blasted forever; she can stand no longer, as a free Republican Government, but must fall to rise no more.

With these brief remarks we shall suit will be hailed as a welcome guest, by every lover of freedom, and receive that encouragement which its merits may demand.

E. ROBINSON, D. C. SMITH.

Extract,

FROM THE PRIVATE JOURNAL OF JOSEPH SMITH JR.

On the fourteenth day of March, in the year of our Lord one thousand eight hundred and thirty eight, I with my family, arrived in Far West, Caldwell county Missouri, after a journey of more then one thousand miles, in the, Winter season, and being about eight weeks on our Journey; during which we suffered great affliction, and met with considerable persecution on the road. However, the prospect of meeting my friends in the west and anticipating the pleasure of dwelling in peace, and enjoying the blessings thereof, buoyed me up under the difficulties and trials which I had then to endure. However, I had not been there long before I was given to understand that plots were laid, by wicked and designing men for my destruction, who sought every opportunity to take my life; and that a company on the Grindstone forks of Grand river, in the county of Daviess, had offered the sum of one thousand dollars for my scalp: persons of whom I had no knowledge whatever, and who, I suppose, were entire strangers to me; and in order to accomplish their wicked design, I was frequently waylaid &c.; consequently, my life was continually in jeopardy:

I could hardly have given credit to such statements, had they not been corroborated by testimony, the most strong and convincing; as shortly after my arrival at Far West, while watering my horse in Shoal Creek, I distinctly heard three or four guns snap, which were undoubtedly intended for my destruction; however, I was mercifully preserved from those who sought to destroy me, by their lurking in the woods and hiding places, for this purpose.

My enemies were not confined alone, to the ignorant and obscure, but men in office, and holding situations under the Governor of the State, proclaimed themselves my enemies, and gave encouragement to others to destroy me; amongst whom, was Judge King, of the fifth Judicial circuit, who has frequently been heard to say that I ought to be beheaded on account of my religion. Expressions such as these, from individuals holding such important offices as Judge King's, could not fail to produce, and encourage persecution against me, and the people with whom I was connected. And in consequence of the prejudice which existed in the mind of this Judge, which he did not endeavor to keep secret, but made it as public as he could, the people took every advantage they possibly could, in abusing me, and threatening my life; regardless of the laws, which promise protection to every religious society, without distinction.

During this state of things I do not recollect that either myself, or the people with whom I was associated, had done anything to deserve such treatment, but felt a desire to live at peace, and on friendly terms, with the. citizens of that, and the adjoining counties, as well as with all men; and I can truly say "for my love they were my enemies," and "sought to slay me without any cause," or the least shadow of pretext.

My family was kept in a state of alarm, not knowing, when I went from home, that I should ever return again; or what would befall me from day to day. But notwithstanding these manifestations of enmity, I hoped that the citizens would eventually cease from their abusive and murderous purposes, and would reflect with sorrow upon their conduct in endeavoring to destroy me, whose only crime was in worshipping the God of heaven, and keeping his commandments; and that they would soon desist from harassing a people who were as good citizens as the majority of this vast republic-who labored almost night and day, to cultivate the ground; and whose industry, during the time they were in that neighborhood, was proverbial.

In the latter part of September, A. D. 1838, I took a journey, in company with some others, to the lower part of the county of Caldwell, for the purpose of selecting a location for a Town. While on my journey, I was met by one of our brethren from Dewitt, in Carroll county, who stated that our people, who had settled in that place, were, and had been for some time, surrounded by a mob, who had threatened their lives and had shot at them several times; and that he was on his way to Far West, to inform the brethren there, of the facts. I was surprised on receiving this intelligence, although there had, previous to this time, been some manifestations of mobs, but I had hoped that the good sense of the majority of the people, and their respect for the constitution, would have put down any spirit of persecution, which might have been manifested in that neighborhood.

Immediately on receiving this intelligence, I made preparations to go to that place, and endeavor if possible, to allay the feelings of the citizens, and save the lives of my brethren who were thus exposed to their wrath. I arrived at Dewitt, about the first of October, and found that the accounts of the situation of that place were correct, for it was with much difficulty, and by travelling [traveling] unfrequented roads, that I was able to get there; all the principal roads being strongly guarded by the mob, who refused all ingress as well as egress. I found my brethren, (who were only a handfull [handful] , in comparison to the mob, by which they were surrounded,) in this situation, and their provisions nearly exhausted, and no prospect of obtaining any more.

We thought it necessary to send immediately to the Governor, to inform him of the circumstances; hoping, from the Executive, to receive the protection which we needed, and which was guaranteed to us, in common with other citizens. Several Gentlemen of standing and respectability, who lived in the immediate vicinity, (who were not in any wise connected with the church of Latter Day Saints,) who had witnessed the proceedings of our enemies; came forward and made affidavits to the treatment we had received, and concerning our perilous situation; and offered their services to go and present the case to the Governor themselves. A messenger was accordingly despatched to his Excellency, who made known to him our situation. But instead of receiving any aid whatever, or even sympathy from his Excellency, we were told that "the quarrel was between the Mormons and the mob," and that "we might fight it out." In the mean time, we had petitioned the Judges to protect us. They sent out about one hundred of the militia,. under the command of Brigadier General Parks; but almost immediately on their arrival, General Parks informed us that the greater part of his men under Capt. Bogart had mutinied, and that he shoud [should] be obliged to draw them off from the place, for fear they would join the mob; consequently he could afford us no assistance.

We had now, no hopes whatever, of successfully resisting the mob, who kept constantly increasing: our provisions were entirely exhausted and we being wearied out, by continually standing on guard, and watching the movements of our enemies; who, during the time I was there, fired at us a great many times. Some of the brethren died, for want of the common necessaries of life, and perished from starvation; and for once in my life, I had the pain of beholding some of my fellow creatures fall victims to the spirit of persecution, which did then and has since prevailed to such an extent in Upper Missouri-men too, who were virtuous, and against whom, no legal process could for one moment, be sustained; but who, in consequence of their love to God-attachment to his cause- and there determination to keep the faith were thus brought to an untimely grave.

Many houses belonging to my brethren, were burned; their cattle driven away, and a great quantity of their property destroyed by the mob. Seeing no prospect of relief, the Governor having turned a deaf ear to our entreaties, the militia having mutinied, and the greater part of them ready to join the mob; the brethren came to the conclusion to leave that place, and seek a shelter elsewhere; they consequently took their departure, with about seventy waggons, with the remnant of the property they had been able to save from their matchless foes, and proceeded to Caldwell. During our journey, we were continually harrassed and threatened by the mob, who shot at us several times; whilst several of our brethren died from the fatigue and privations which they had to endure, and we had to inter them by the wayside, without a coffin, and under circumstances the most distressing.

On my arrival in Caldwell I was informed by General Doniphan of Clay county, that a company of mobbers eight hundred strong, were marching towards a settlement of our people's in Daviess county. He ordered out one of the officers to raise a force and march immediately to what he called Wight's town and defend our people from the attacks of the mob, until he should raise the militia in his, and the adjoining counties to put them down. A small company of militia who were on their route to Daviess county, and who had passed through Far West, he ordered back again, stating that they were not to be depended upon, as many of them were disposed to join the mob; and to use his own expression, were "damned rotten hearted." According to orders Lieut. Colonel Hinkle marched with a number of our people to Daviess county to afford what assistance they could to their brethren. Having some property in that county and having a house building there, I went up at the same time. While I was there a number of houses belonging to our people were burned by the mob, who committed many other depredations, such as driving off horses, sheep, cattle hogs &c. A number, whose houses were burned down as well as those who lived in scattered and lonely situations, fled into the town for safety, and for shelter from the inclemency of the weather, as a considerable snow storm had taken place just about that time; women and children, some in the most delicate situations, were thus obliged to leave their homes, and travel several miles in order to effect their escape. My feelings were such as I cannot describe when I saw the flock in the village, almost entirely destitute of clothes, and only escaping with their lives. During this state of affairs General Parks arrived at Daviess county, and was at the house of Colonel Wight, when the intelligence was brought, that the mob were burning houses; and also when women and children were fleeing for safety. Colonel Wight who held a commission the 59th regiment under his (General Parks) command, asked what was to be done. He told him that he must immediately, call out his men and go and put them down. Accordingly, a force was immediately raised for the purpose of quelling the mob, and in a short time were on their march with a determination to drive the mob, or die in the attempt; as they could bear such treatment no longer. The mob having learned the orders of General Parks, and likewise being aware of the determination of the oppressed, they broke up their encampments and fled.

The mob seeing that they could not succeed by force, now resorted to stratagem; and after removing their property out of their houses, which were nothing but log cabins, they actually set fire to their own houses, and then reported to the authorities of the state that the Mormons were burning and destroying all before them.

On the retreat of the mob from Daviess, I returned to Caldwell, hoping to have some respite from our enemies, at least for a short time; but upon my arrival there, I was informed that a mob had commenced hostilities on the borders of that county, adjoining to Ray co. and that they had taken some of our brethren prisoners, burned some houses and had committed depredations on the peaceable inhabitants. A company under the command of Capt. Patten, was ordered out by Lieutenant Col. Hinckle to go against them, and stop their depredations, and drive them out of the county. Upon the approach of our people, the mob fired upon them, and after discharging their pieces, fled with great precipitation, with the loss of one killed and several wounded. In the engagement Capt. Patten, (a man beloved by all who had the pleasure of his acquaintance,) was wounded and died shortly after. Two others were likewise killed and several wounded. Great excitement now prevailed, and mobs were heard of in every direction who seemed determined on our destruction. They burned the houses in the country and took off all the cattle they could find. They destroyed cornfields, took many prisoners, and threatened death to all the Mormons. On the 28 of Oct. a large company of armed soldiery were seen aproaching [approaching] Far West. They came up near to the town and then drew back about a mile and encamped for the night. We were informed that they were Militia, ordered out by the Governor for the purpose of stopping our proceedings; it having been represented to his excellency, by wicked and designing men from Daviess, that we were the aggressors, and had committed outrages in Daviess &c. They had not yet got the Governors orders of *extermination*, which I believe did not arrive until the next day. On the following morning, a flag was sent, which was met by several of our people, and it was hoped that matters would be satisfactorily arranged after the officers had heard a true statement of all the circumstances. Towards evening, I was waited upon by Colonel Hinckle who stated that the officers of the Militia desired to have an interview with me, and some others, hoping that the difficulties might be settled without having occasion to carry into effect the exterminating orders, which they had received from the Governor. I immediately complied with the request, and in company with Elders Rigdon and Pratt, Colonel Wight, and Geo. W. Robinson, went into the camp of the militia. But judge of my surprise, when instead of being treated with that respect which is due from one citizen to another, we were taken as prisoners of war, and were treated with the utmost contempt. The officer would not converse with us, and the soldiers, almost to a man, insulted us as much as they felt disposed, breathing out threats against me and my companions. I cannot begin to tell the scene which I there witnessed. The loud cries and yells of more than one thousand voices, which rent the air and could be heard for miles; and the horrid and blasphemous threats and curses which were poured upon us in torrents, were enough to appal [appall] the stoutest heart. in the evening we had to lie down on the cold ground surrounded by a strong guard, who were only kept back by the power of God from depriving us of life. We petitioned the officers to know why we were thus treated, but they utterly refused to give us any answer, or to converse with us. The next day they held a court martial, and sentenced us to be shot, on Friday morning, on the public square, as an ensample [example] to the Mormons. However notwithstanding their sentence,. and determination, they were not permitted to carry their murderous sentence into execution.

Having an opportunity of speaking to General Wilson, I inquired of him the cause why I was thus treated, I told him I was not sensible of having done any thing worthy of such treatment; that I had always been a supporter of the constitution and of Democracy. His answer was 'I know it, and that is the reason why I want to kill you or have you killed." The militia then went into the town and without any restrain whatever, plundered the houses, and abused the innocent and unoffending inhabitants. They went to my house and drove my family out of doors. They carried away most of my property and left many destitute.-We were taken to the town, into the public square; and before our departure from Far West, we, after much entreaties, were suffered to see our families, being attended all the while with a strong guard; I found my wife and children in tears, who expected we were shot by those who had sworn to take our lives, and that they should see me no more. When I entered my house, they clung to my garments, their eyes streaming with tears, while mingled emotions of joy and sorrow were manifest in their countenances. I requested to have a private interview with them a few minutes, but this privilege was denied me. I was then obliged to take my departure, but who can realize my feelings which I experienced at that time; to be torn from my companion, and leaving her surrounded with monsters in the shape of men, and my children too, not knowing how their wants would be supplied; to be taken far from them in order that my enemies might destroy me when they thought proper to do so. My partner wept, my children clung to me and were only thrust from my by the swords of the guard who guarded me. I felt overwhelmed while I witnessed the scene, and could only recommend them to the care of that God, whose kindness had followed me to the present time; and who alone could protect them and deliver me from the hands of my enemies and restore me to my family.

I was then taken back to the camp and then I with the rest of my brethren, viz: Sidney Rigdon, Hyram Smith, Parley P. Pratt, Lyman Wight, Amasa Lyman, and George W. Robinson, were removed to Independence, Jackson county. They did not make known what their intention or designs were in taking us there; but knowing that some of our most bitter enemies resided in that county, we came to the conclusion that their design was to shoot us, which from the testimony of others; I do think was a correct conclusion. While there, we were under the care of Generals Lucas and Wilson, we had to find our own board, and had to sleep on the floor with nothing but a mantle for our covering, and a stick of wood for our pillow. After remaining there a few days we were ordered by General Clark to return; we were accordingly taken back as far as Richmond, and there we were thrust into prison and our feet bound with fetters. While in Richmond, we were under the charge of Colonel Price from Chariton county, who suffered all manner of abuse to be heaped upon us. During this time my afflictions were great, and our situation was truly painful. After remaining there a few days we were taken before the court of inquiry, but were not prepared with witnesses, in cousequence [consequence] of the cruelty of the mob, who threatened destruction to all who had any thing to say in our favor: but notwithstanding their threats there were a few who did not think their lives dear so that they might testify to the truth, and in our behalf, knowing we were unlawfully confined; but the court who was predjudiced [prejudiced] against us, would not suffer them to be examined according to law, but suffered the State's Attorney to abuse them as he thought proper. We were then removed to Liberty jail in Clay county, and there kept in close confinement in that place for more than four months. While there, we petitioued [petitioned] Judge Turnham for a writ of habeas corpus, but on account of the predjudice [prejudiced] of the jailor [jailer] all communication was cut off; at length however, we succeeded in getting a petition conveyed to him, but for fourteen days we received no answer. We likewise petitioned the other Judges but with no success. After the expiration of fourteen days Judge Turnham ordered us to appear before him, we sent and took a number of witnesses, which caused us considerable expense and trouble; but he altogether refused to hear any of our witnesses. The lawyers which we had employed refused to act; being afraid of the people. This being the case, we of course could not succeed, and were consequently remanded back to our prison house.-We were sometimes visited by ours friends whose kindness and attention, I shall ever remember with feelings of lively gratitude, but frequently we were not suffered to have that privilege. Our vituals [food] were of the coarsest kind, and served up in a manner which was disgusting. We continued in this situation, bearing up under the injuries and cruelties we suffered as well as we could, until we were removed to Daviess county, where we were taken in order to be tried for the crimes with which we had been charged. The grand jury (who were mostly intoxicated,) indicted us for treason, &c. &c.

While there, we got a change of venue to Boon county, and were conducted on our way to that place by a strong guard. The second evening after our departure the guard got intoxicated, we thought it a favorable opportunity to make our escape; knowing that the only object of our enemies was our destruction; and likewise knowing that a number of our brethren had been massacred by them on Shoal creek, amongst whom were two children; and that they sought every opportunity to abuse others who were left in that state; and that they were never brought to an account for their barbarous proceedings, but were winked at, and encouraged, by those in authority. We thought that it was necessary for us, inasmuch as we loved our lives, and did not wish to die by the hand of murderers and assasins [assassins]; and inasmuch, as we loved our families and friends, to deliver ourselves from our enemies, and from that land of tyrany [tyranny] and oppression, and again take our stand among a people in whose bosoms dwell those feelings of republicanism and liberty which gave rise to our nation:-Feelings which the inhabitants of the state of Missouri were strangers to.-Accordingly we took the advantage of the situation of our guard and took our departure, and that night we travled [traveled] a considerable distance. We continued on our journey both by night and by day, and after suffering much fatigue and hunger, I arrived in Quincy Illinois, amidst the congratulations of my friends and the embraces of my family.

I have now resided in this neighborhood for several weeks as it is known to thousands of the citizens of Illinois, as well as of the State of Missouri, but the authorities of Mo., knowing that they had no justice in their crusade against me, and the people with whom I was associated, have not yet to my knowledge, taken the first step towards having me arrested.

Amongst those who have been the chief instruments, and leading characters, in the unparallelled [unparalleled]] persecutions against the church of Latter Day Saints; the following stand conspicuous, viz: General Clark, Wilson, and Lucas, Colonel Price, and Cornelius Guilliam. Captain Bogart also, whose zeal in the cause of oppression and injustice, was unequalled [unequaled], and whose delight has been to rob, murder, and spread devastation amongst the Saints. He stole a valuable horse, saddle and bridle from me; which cost two hundred dollars, and then sold the same to General Wilson. On understanding this I applied to General Wilson for the horse, who assured me, upon the honor of a gentleman, and an officer, that I should have the horse returned to me; but this promise has not been fulfilled.

All the threats, murders, and robberies which these, officers have been guilty of, are entirely looked over by the Executive of the state; who, to hide his own iniquity, must of course shield and protect those whom he employed, to cary [carry] into effect his murderous purposes.

I was in their hands as a prisoner about six months, but notwithstanding their determination to destroy me, with the rest of my brethren who were with me; and although at three different times (as I was informed) we were sentenced to be shot, without the least shadow of law, (as we were not military men,) and had the time, and place appointed for that purpose; yet through the mercy of God, in answer to the prayers of the saints, I have been preserved, and delivered out of their hands, and can again enjoy the society of my friends and brethren, whom I love: and to whom I feel united in bonds that are stronger than death: and in a state where I believe the laws are respected, and whose citizens, are humane and charitable.

During the time I was in the hands of my enemies; I must say, that although I felt great anxiety, respecting my family and friends; who were so inhumanly [inhumanely] treated and abused; and who had to mourn the loss of their husbands and children, who had been slain; and after having been robbed of nearly all that they possessed be driven from their homes, and forced to wander as strangers in a strange country, in order, that they might save themselves and their little ones, from, the destructions they were threatened with in Missouri: yet as far as I was concerned, I felt perfectly calm, and resigned to the will of my heavenly Father. I knew my innocency, as well as that of the saints; and that we had done nothing to deserve such treatment from the hands of our oppressors: consequently, I could took to that God, who has the hearts of all men in his hands, and who had saved me frequently from the gates of death for deliverance: and notwithstanding, that every avenue of escape seemed to be entirely closed, and death stared me in the face, and that my destruction was determined upon, as far as man was concerned; yet, from my first entrance into the camp, I felt an assurance, that I with my brethren and our families should be delivered. Yes, that still small voice, which has so often whispered consolation to my soul, in the debth [depth] of sorrow and distress, bade me be of good cheer, and promised deliverance which gave me great comfort: and although, the heathen raged, and the people imagined vain things, yet the Lord of hosts, the God of Jacob, was my refuge; and when I cried unto him in the day of trouble, he delivered me; for which I call upon my soul, and all that is within me, to bless and praise his holy name: For although I was "troubled on every side, yet not distressed; perplexed, but not in despair; persecuted, but not forsaken; cast down, but not destroyed."

The conduct of the saints under their accumulated wrongs and suffering, has been praise-worthy; their courage, in defending their brethren from the ravages of mobs; their attachment to the cause of truth, under circumstances the most trying and distressing which humanity can possibly endure; their love to each other; their readiness to afford assistance to me, and my brethren who were confined in a dungeon; their sacrifices in leaving the state of Missouri, and assisting the poor widows and orphans, and securing them houses in a more hospitable land; all conspire to raise them in the estimation of all good and virtuous men; and has secured them the favor and approbation of Jehovah; and a name, as imperishable as eternity. And their virtuous deeds, and heroic actions, while in defence of truth and their brethren: will be fresh and blooming; when the names of their oppressors shall either be entirely forgotten, or only remembered, for their barbarity and cruelty. Their attention and affection to me, while in prison, will ever be remembered hen they came to do any kind offices, and to cheer our minds while we were in the gloomy prison house, gave me feelings, which I cannot describe, while those who wished to insult and abuse us, by their threats and blasphemous language, were applauded and had every encouragement given them.

However, thank God, we have been delivered; and although, some of our beloved brethren, have had to seal their testimony with their blood; and have died martyrs to the cause of truth; yet,

Short, though bitter was their pain,

Everlasting is their joy.

Let us not sorrow as "those without hope," the time is fast approaching, when we shall see them again, and rejoice together, without being affraid [afraid] of wicked men: Yes, those who have slept in Christ, shall be bring with him, when he shall come to be glorified in his saints, and admired by all those who believe: but to take vengeance upon his enemies, and all those who obey not the gospel. At that time, the hearts of the widow and fatherless shall be comforted, and every tear shall be wiped from of their faces.

The trials they have had to pass through, shall work together for their good, and prepare them for the society of those, who have come up out of great tribulation; and have washed their robes, and made them white in the blood of the Lamb. Marvel not then, if you are persecuted, but remember the words of the Savior, "The servant is not above his Lord, if they have persecuted, me, they will persecute you also;" and that all the afflictions through which the saints have to pass, are in fulfillment of the words of the prophets, which have spoken since the world began. We shall therfore [therefore] do well to discern the signs of the times, as we pass along, that the day of the Lord may not "overtake us as a thief in the night." Affliction, persecutions, imprisonments and deaths, we must expect according to the scriptures, which tell us, that the blood of those whose souls were under the alter, could not be avenged on them that dwell on the earth, untill [until] their brethren should be slain, as they were.

If these transactions had taken place among barbarrians [barbarians], under the authority of a despot; or in a nation, where a certain religion is established according to law, and all others proscribed; then there might have been some shadow of defence offered. But can we realize that in a land which is the cradle of Liberty and equal rights, and where the voice of the conquerers [conquerors], who had vanquished our foes, had scarcely died away upon our ears, where we frequently mingled with those who had stood amidst the "battle and the breeze," and whose arms have been nerved in the defence of their country and liberty: whose institutions are the theme of philosophers and poets, and held up to the admiration of the whole civilized world. In the midst of all these scenes, with which we were surrounded a persecution, the most unwarrantable, was commenced; and a tragedy, the most dreadful, was enacted, by a large portion of the inhabitants, of one of those free and independent States, which comprise this vast republic; and a deadly blow was struck at the institutions, for which our Fathers had fought many a hard battle, and for which, many a Patriot had shed his blood; and suddenly, was heard, amidst the voice of joy and gratitude for our national liberty, the voice of mourning, lamentation and woe. Yes, in this land a mob, regardless of those laws, for which so much blood had been spilled, dead to every feeling of virtue and patriotism, which animated the bosom of freemen; fell upon a people whose religious faith was different from their own; and not only destroyed their homes, drove them away, and carried off their property, but murderd [murdered] many a free born son of America. A tragedy, which has no parrallel [parallel] in modern, and hardly in ancient times; even the face of the Red man would be ready to turn pale at the recital of it.

It would have been some consolation, if the authorities of the State had been innocent in this affair, but they are involved in the guilt thereof; and the blood of innocence, even of *children*, cry for vengeance upon them. I ask the citizens of this vast republic, whether such a state of things is to be suffered to pass unnoticed, and the hearts of widows, orphans and patriots, to be broken, and their wrongs left without redress? No! I invoke the genius of our constitution, I appeal to the patriotism of Americans, to stop this unlawful and unholy procedure: and pray that God may defend this nation from the dreadful effects of such outrages. Is there not virtue in the body politic? Will not the people rise up in their majesty, and with that promptitude and zeal, which is so characterestic [characteristic] of them, discountenance such proceedings, by bringing the offenders to that punishment which they so richly deserve; and save the nation from that disgrace and ultimate ruin, which otherwise must inevitably fall upon it? JOSEPH SMITH JR.

Payson, Ill., June 18th. 1839.

Messrs. Robinson and Smith:

Having learned that you intend to publish a monthly periodical, called the Times and Seasons, for the purpose of giving general information concerning the work of the Lord, at home and abroad, thinking that it might be a satisfaction to the saints, in general, to know of the prosperity of our Redeemer's kingdom in the eastern country; I have thought proper to send you a short history of my travels during the last year: if you deem it worthy of an insertion in the above named paper, it is at your disposal.

I left Ohio the last of Jan. 1838, with a view of proclaiming the fulness [fullness] of the everlasting gospel to the inhabitants of the eastern country. I spent from three to four months time, preaching in Washington Co. Md. and Franklin, Bedford and Huntington counties, Pa. during which time I preached from 80 to 100 times; held one debate; and several times defended the truth publicly, when attacked by the priests of the different denominations; baptized one, and witnessed the baptism of many others, by elders who were laboring with me.

June first I pursued my Journey eastward preaching as I went. On the 7th of July I arrived at a small town called Hornerstown, Monmouth co. N. J. I then obtained the liberty of the school house in that place, and made an appointment for the next day. At this time, if I have correct information, there had never been but two or three sermons, of this doctrine, preached in that state; consequently, as to our principles, and rules of faith, the people knew nothing, except by reports. After I had fulfilled the appointment which I had made by setting forth the first principles of the doctrine of Christ, it was so different from what they had expected, that it caused a spirit of inquiry, so much so, that I had calls in every direction. I then sent appointments to different places in the county, and commenced fulfilling them; the people flocked out, in crowds to hear, yet at this time, more out of curiosity than any thing else; and in a short time, the news went abroad, that a Mormon preacher had made his appearance in the land; and the more I preached, the greater the excitement, so that in every town, and neighborhood, where I had preached, what the world calls Mormonism, was the grand topic of conversation. The honest in heart exclaiming that it was truth, while another class of the community, who loves darkness more that light, lifted their voices and influence against it; some saying that I preached from another bible, different from our common version; but the honest in heart, searched the scriptures, and learned to the contrary. At this particular crises, while the honest were searching the scriptures, the priests were engaged in fumbling over their old news paper files, and hunting up all the old stories that was told a number of years ago, probably thinking that this would be the most effectual way to stop the spread of truth. After they had gathered the old news paper stories and reports that had been put in circulation, by our enemies, three priests, a Methodist, Baptist and Universalist, united, Pilate and Herod like, to combat the truth.

At this time I had an appointment at a place called New Egypt; they gave out word, which had a general circulation throughout the country, that on the evening of the appointment, Mormonism would be exposed, and the arguments adduced in its favor, refuted; and that I should be put to shame. On the evening of the appointment the people flocked into the town, from every direction: I walked the streets, before the appointed hour for meeting, and heard the people conversing about the subject of controversy, and found that their expectations were, to hear a scriptural argument; the meeting commenced, and I addressed the congregation upon the subject of the Millennium, as long as I thought proper, and then gave liberty; the Methodist preacher arose, and said that he had a number of questions written down, which he wished me to answer; I told him that if they were reasonable ones, I would answer them. The first question was this, what is Mormonism, and will any person be saved if they reject it?-I told him I could soon answer that question. My answer was this, Mormonism, as you call it, is to believe that Christ is the Son of God, also a firm belief in the scriptures, then faith, repentance and baptism for the remission of sins: the laying on of hands for the reception of the Holy Ghost, having a church organized according to the new testament pattern, and to live by every word that proceeds from the mouth of God; all who reject this will be damned, if the scriptures are true. As to the other questions, they were as easy answered as that of the first. They then commenced repeating news paper stories, reading a pamphlet, and telling all the tales that they had heard with foul insinuations, and in a sarcastick [sarcastic] manner, made use of invective appalations [appellations] to blast the characters of men, whom God had raised up for the purpose of bringing about his great and marvelous work of the last days; probably thinking that by so doing, it would render the society, and its principles, odious in the minds of the people, so that they would stop their ears, and cease to hear any more. As for myself, my determination ever has been, not to partake of the spirit of slander, and of a strife of this kind; but when the truth is attacked I always feel bound to boldly defend it; neither had I any disposition for a controversy of this kind; consequently, I bore testimony to the truth of the doctrine that I had proclaimed: and showed that their news paper stories were false, and that they were hatched up by evil designing men, to destroy the work of truth: I then dismissed the meeting.

Those who were opposed to the truth, who came with anticipations of a general triumph over Mormonism, and that I would be put to shame, and forced to abandon the country with disgrace; instead of rejoicing, on the account of successful labors, were astonished at the conduct of the priests, and returned home with amazement, more than rejoicing, others knowing that slander, was no argument, and that there had no argument been adduced, to overthrow the doctrine that I had proclaimed, acknowledged that there was no scriptural argument that could be produced to overthrow it, and those who made the attack, instead of putting me to shame, they put themselves to shame; and instead of exposing Mormonism, they exposed their own wickedness; rendered themselves odious in the minds of the most of the congregation; so that their influence against Mormonism was but little, after that. After this, they no more attempted to expose Mormonism, publicly, where I had a chance to defend it; but commenced warning their members not to go and hear, telling them, that they would get bewitched, or led astray, or deceived; (what better testimony do we want, to prove that they are on a sandy foundation, for if they are built upon the rock, the gates of hell cannot prevail against them;)

yet, notwithstanding all their exertions to destroy Mormonism, the people believed it more than ever, for this reason, they had made their assertions, that Mormonism was an unscriptural doctrine, and that they could make it appear so, but when the time of trial came, they failed in the attempt; and, as my manner of teaching was, to reason from the scriptures, the honest were constrained to acknowledge, that there is no scripture to condemn it.-And as I continued preaching, the prejudices of the people wore away, and there was a general spirit of inquiry. The rich and the poor, invited me to their homes, that they might learn the particulars concerning this work.

Thus I continued laboring and making the things of God plain to their understandings; some weeks preaching as often as ten or eleven times. The last of September, Elder O. Pratt came from the city of N. Y. and preached in this region of country several times, which was the means of doing much good.

On the 1st of Oct. a number came forward, and embraced the fullness of the everlasting gospel, by obeying the ordinance of baptism. I continued preaching and baptizing, till the last of Dec. when I called the saints together, at Hornerstown, in order to organize a branch of the church in that place. Josiah Ells, (formerly a Methodist preacher,) was set apart by the voice of the members, and ordained to the office of an Elder; the work of the Lord still rolled on.

January 28th., 1839, I took my leave of the saints, which then numbered 26, to go to the State of Mo. I went as far as Lightersburgh, Md. where I got more particular information of the late persecution in the State of Mo.-I then concluded, that my labors would be of more use in the world, than at home; consequently, after preaching several times to the saints in Lightersburgh, I returned to the State of N. J. with a view of again proclaiming the truth, to the people of that state. By request of some of the citizens, I went to preach, in a town called Toms River, situated near the sea shore; some members of certain sect, in the place locked up the school house. A congregation assembled, and with them, some noble minded men, who had an independent spirit; the door was opened, and I preached to an attentive congregation. I preached several times in the place, and baptized 11 persons. April 1st, elders L. Barnes and H. Sagers visited the branch of the church in that State, and preached several times, as they were on the way to the city of N. Y. They told me that they had been preaching in Chester Co. Pa. and had baptized four, and they thought that there was a foundation laid, for a still greater work.-On elder Barnes' return from the city, he held a debate with a Quaker preacher, and nobly defended the truth, he preached several times in that region of country, and baptized 5, then returned to Pa. On the 9th of May, I took my leave of the saints in that State, to come to Illinois. I find by looking over my Journal, that since I commenced laboring in the State of N. J. which was chiefly confined to Monmouth, Burlington and Mercer counties, that I have preached 200 sermons, baptized 40 persons, visited the saints in the city of N. Y. several times; and I feel myself authorized to say, that the work of the Lord is gaining ground, in the region of country where I have been laboring.

May the Lord inspire his servants, with a renewed zeal, that they may go forth, and bear a faithful testimony, to the inhabitants of the earth, that this work might hasten on, till all nations shall hear the sound, and until Zion shall become a peaceful home, and peace flow like a river to all the people of God. Yours respectfully, B. Winchester.

TIMES AND SEASONS

COMMERCE, ILL. NOV. 1839

A WORD TO THE SAINTS.

It may be expected by some, who are not acquainted with all the circumstances attending the printing establishment had in the church, that the proprietors of this press should supply the subscribers of the "Elders Journal," with the remaining numbers of that paper, which was their due when we were broken up by the mob in Missouri; but this idea we are confident they will abandon, when they learn the fact, that the proprietors of the Journal, while conducting that paper, sustained the loss of anentire [an entire] establishment in Kirtland Ohio, in Jan. 1838, after which, with much difficulty, they procured another press and resuscitated the paper at Far West Mo. where they had the opportunity of publishing two numbers only; when persecution raged to that extent, that they were compelled to leave the State, with the loss of nearly all their property. Thus, while many of you have sustained the loss of but 67 cents, they have not only lost all their property, but have been driven by their cruel and hard-hearted persecutors, from their peaceful and happy homes, and are now strangers, sojourning in a strange land; which verifies the saying of the Savior, when speaking to his disciples, where he says, "if ye were of the world, the world would love his own, but because ye are not of the world; but I have chosen you out of the world, therefore the world hateth you."

But notwithstanding all these circumstances, being partakers in the deep afflictions through which the saints were called to pass in Missouri, we have been permitted, by the blessing of heaven, to obtain the necessary apparatus, and will publish, for the benefit of the saints, a monthly paper, which we now offer to them on reasonable terms; but owing to our peculiar circumstances, we shall be under the necessity of requiring pay on subscriptions, in advance, as our expenses are, necessarily, very heavy, and nothing but cash in hand will defray them; however, as it is not generally known, that this paper is to be published, we shall forward this number to such as we are confident feel an interest in the gathering of Israel, and the accomplishment of that glorious work which the Lord has commenced in these last days, with the expectation that they will, upon the receipt of this, forward us their names with the money, free of postage, as it will not be in our power, (notwithstanding, it would be pleasing to us, to do otherwise,) to forward any more, until remittances are made; and we earnestly hope that the saints will not think hard of us for being thus partiular [particular], as it is the only principle upon which we can sustain this publication.

-> In our next, we shall commence publishing the history of the disturbances in Missouri, in regular series.

To the elders of the church of Jesus Christ of Latter Day Saints, to the churches scattered abroad, and to all the saints.

We, the undersigned, feeling deeply interrested [interested] in the welfare of Zion, the up-building of the church of Christ, and the welfare of the saints in general, send unto you GREETING:-and pray, that "grace, mercy, and peace may rest upon you, from God our Father, and from our Lord Jesus Christ."

But brethren, the situation of things, as they have of late existed, have been to us of a peculiar trying nature. Many of you have been driven from you homes, robbed of your possessions, and deprived of the liberty of conscience; you have been stripped of your clothing, plundering of your furniture, robbed of your horses, your cattle, your sheep, your hogs, and refused the protection of law; you have been subject to insult and abuse, from a set of lawless miscreants; you have had to endure cold, nakedness, peril, and sword; your wives and your children, have been deprived of the comforts of life; you have been subject to bonds, to imprisonment, to banishment, and many to death, "for the testimony of Jesus, and for the word of God." Many of your brethren, with those whose souls are now beneath the alter, are crying for the vengence [vengeance] of heaven to rest upon the heads of their devoted murderers, and saying, "how long O Lord, holy and true, dost thou not judge and avenge our blood on them that dwell on the earth;" but is was said to them, "that they should rest, yet for a little season, until their fellow servants also; and their brethren, that should be killed as THEY WERE should be fulfilled." Dear brethren, we should remind you of this thing, and although you have had indignities, insults and injuries heaped upon you, till further suffering would seem to be no longer a virtue we would say, be patient, dear brethren, for as saith the apostle, "ye have need of patience, that after being tried have been tried you may inherit the promise." You have been tried in the furnace of affliction, the time to exercise patience is now come; and "we shall reap, brethren, in *due time* if we faint not." Do not breathe vengeance upon your oppressors, but leave the case in the hands of God, "for vengeance is mine, saith the Lord, and I will repay."

We would say to the widow, and to the orphan, to the destitute, and to the diseased, who have been made so through persecution *be patient*, you are not forgotten, the God of Jacob has his eye upon you, the heavens have been witness to your sufferings, and they are registered on high; angels have gazed upon the scene, and your tears, your groans, your sorrows, and anguish of heart, are had in remembrance before God; they have entered into the sympathies of that bosom, who is "touched with the feeling of our infirmities," who was "tempted in all points, like unto you;" they have entered into the ears of the Lord of Sabaoth; be patient then, until the words of God be fulfilled, and his designs accomplished and then shall he pour out his vengeance upon the devoted heads of your murderers, and then shall they know that he is God, and that you are his people.

And we would say to all the saints who have made a covenant with the Lord by sacrifice, that inasmuch as you are faithful, you shall not lose your reward, although not numbered among those who were in the late difficulties in the west.

We swish to stimulate all the brethren to faithfulness; you have been tried, you are now being tried, and those trials, if you are not watchful, will corode [corrode] upon the mind, and produce unpleasant feelings; but recollect that now is the time of trial, soon the victory will be ours; now may be a day of lamentation, then will be a day of rejoicing; now may be a day of sorrow, but by and by we shall see our Lord, our sorrow will be turned into joy, and our joy no man taketh from us. Be honest; be men of truth and integrity, let your word be your bond, be diligent, be prayerful; pray for, and with your families, train up your children in the fear of the Lord, cultivate a meek a quiet spirit, clothe the naked, feed the hungry, help the destitute, be merciful to the widow and orphan, be merciful to your brethren, and to all men; bear with one anothers infirmities, considering your own weakness; bring no railing accusation against your brethren, especially take care that you do not against the authorities or, elders of the church, for the principle is of the devil; he is called the accuser of the brethren; and Michael, the Arch-angel dared not bring a railing accusation against the devil, but said, the "Lord rebuke thee Satan;" and any man who pursues this course of accusation and murmuring, will fall into the snare of the devil, and apostatize, except he repent. Jude, in the 8th verse. says, likewise those filthy dreamers despise dominion, and speak evil of dignities; and says he, behold, the Lord cometh with ten thousand of his saints, to execute judgement [judgment] upon the ungodly, and to convince all that are ungodly among them, of all their ungodly deeds which they have ungodly committed, and of all their hard *speeches* which ungodly sinners have spoken against him. Peter, in speaking on the same principle, says, "the Lord knoweth how to deliver the godly out of temptations, and to reserve the unjust unto the day of judgement [judgment] to be punished: but chiefly them that walk after the flesh in the lust of uncleanness, and despise government. Presumptous [Presumptuous]*are they* self willed, they are not afraid to *speak evil of dignities.* Whereas angels, which are greater in power and might, bring not railing accusation against them before the Lord." If a man sin, let him be dealt with according to the law of God in the bible, the book of Mormon, and doctrines and covenants, and then leave him in the hands of God to rebuke, as Michael left the devil.

Gird yourselves with righteousness, and let truth, eternal truth, be written indelibly on your hearts. Pray for the prosperity of Zion, for the prophet and his counsellors [counselors] , for the twelve, the high council, the high priests, the seventies, the elders, the bishops, and all the saints, that God may bless them, and preserve his people in righteousness, and grant unto them wisdom and intelligence, that his kingdom may roll forth.

We would say to the elders, that God has called you to an important office, he has laid upon you an onerous duty, he has called you to an holy calling, even to the priests of the "most high God," messengers to the nations of the earth; and upon your diligence, your perseverance and faithfulness, the soundness of the doctrines that you preach, the moral precepts that you advance and practice, and upon the sound principles that you inculcate, hang the destinies of the human family, while you hold that priesthood. You are the men that God has called to spread forth his kingdom, he has committed the care of souls to you charge, and when you received this priesthood, you became the legate of heaven, and the great God demands it of you, that you should be faithful, and inasmuch as you are not, you will not be chosen; but it will be said unto you, stand by, and let a more honorable man than thou art take thy place, and receive thy crown; be careful that you teach not for the word of God, the commandments of men, nor the doctrines of men nor the ordinances of men, inasmuch as you are God's messengers; study the word of God and preach it, and not your opinions, for no man's opinion is worth a straw: advance no principle but what you can prove, for one scriptural proof is worth ten thousand opinions: we would moreover say, abide by that revelation which says, "preach nothing but repentance to this generation," and leave the further mysteries of the kingdom, till God shall tell you to preach them, which is not now.-The horns of the beast, the toes of the image, the frogs and the beast mentioned by John are not going to save this generation, for if a man does not become acquainted with the first principles of the gospel, how shall he understand those greater mysteries, which the most wise cannot understand without revelation. These things therefore, have nothing to do with your mission.

We have heard of some foolish vageries [vagaries], and wild speculations, originating only in a disordered imagination, which are set forth by some, telling what occupation they had before they came into this world, and what they would be employed with after they leave this state of existence; those, and other vain imaginations, we would warn the elders against, because if they listen to such things, they will fall into the snare of the devil, and when the trying time comes, they will be overthrown.

We would also warn the elders, according to previous counsel not to go on to anothers ground without invitation to interfere with another's privilege, for your mission is to the world and not to the churches.

We would also remark, that no man has a right to usurp authority or power over any church, nor has any man power to preside over any church, unless he is solicited and received by the voice of that church to preside.-Preach the first principles of the doctrine of Christ, faith in the Lord Jesus Christ, repentance toward God, baptism in the name of Jesus for the remission of sins, laying on of hands for the gift of the holy Ghost, the resurrection of the dead, and eternal judgement [judgment].

When you go forth to preach, and the Spirit of God rests upon, giving you wisdom and utterance, and enlightning [enlightening] your understanding, be careful that you ascribe the glory to God and not to yourselves; boast not of intelligence, of wisdom, or of power; for it is only that which God has imparted unto you, but be humble, be meek, be patient, and give glory to God.

We would counsel all who have not received a recommend since the difficulties in Mo. to obtain one of the authorities of the church if they wish to be accounted as wise stewards.

We are glad, dear brethren, to see that spirit of enterprise and perseverance which is manifested by you in regard to preaching the gospel; and rejoice to know that neither bonds nor imprisonment, banishment nor exile, poverty or contempt, nor all the combined powers of earth and hell, hinder you from delivering your testimony to the world; and publishing those glad tidings which has been revealed from heaven, by the ministering of angels, by the gift of the holy Ghost, and by the power of God, for the salvation of the world in these last days. And we would say to you, that the hearts of the twelve are with you, and they, with you, are determened [determined] to fulfill their mission, to clear their garments of the blood of this generation, to introduce the gospel to foreign nations, and to make known to the world, those great things which God has developed; they are now on the eve of their departure for England, and will start in a few days, they feel to pray for you, and to solicit an interest in your prayers, and in the prayers of the church, that God, may sustain them in their arduous undertaking; grant them success in their mission, deliver them from the powers of darkness, the stratagems of wicked men, and all the combined powers of earth and hell. And if you, unitedly seek after unity of purpose and design, if you are men of humility, and of faithfulness, of integrity and perseverance, if you submit yourselves to the teachings of heaven, and age guided by the spirit of God, and the salvation of men, and lay your honor prostrate in the dust, if need be, and are willing to fulfil [fulfill] the purses of God in all things; the power of the priesthood will rest upon you, and you will become mighty in testimony: the widow, and the orphan will be made glad, and the poor among men rejoice in the holy one of Israel. Princes will listen to the things that you proclaim, and the nobles of the earth will attend with deference to your words; Queens will rejoice in the glad tidings of salvation, and Kings bow to the sceptre [scepter] of Immanuel; light will burst forth as the morning, and intelligence spread itself as the rays of the sun; the cringing sycophant will be ashamed, and the traitor flee from your presence; superstition, will hide its hoary head, and infidelity be ashamed. And amid the clamour [clamor] of men, the din of war, the rage of pestilence, the commotion of nations, the overthrow of kingdoms and the dissolution of Empires, truth will stalk forth with gigantic strides, and lay hold of the honest in heart among all nations: Zion shall blossom as a rose, and the nations flock to her standard, and the kingdoms of this world shall soon become the kingdoms of our God and of his Christ, and he shall reign for ever and ever, Amen.

BRIGHAM YOUNG, HEBER C. KIMBALL, JOHN E. PAGE, WILFORD WOODRUFF, JOHN TAYLOR, GEORGE A. SMITH.

N. B. We have heard that a man by the name of George M. Hinckle is preaching in the Iowa Territory, we would remark to the public, that we have withdrawn our fellowship from him, and will not stand accountable for any doctrines held forth by him, nor will we be amenable for his conduct. The minutes of a conference will be published mentioning the names of others whom we have withdrawn our fellowship from.

EXTRACTS OF THE MINUTES OF CONFERENCES.

A Conference of the church of Jesus Christ of Latter Day Saints, held in Quincy on the 17th of March, 1839.

Brigham Young was unanimously called to the chair, and Robert B. Thompson chosen clerk. Elder Young then arose and gave a statement of the circumstances of the church at Far West, and his feelings in regard to the scattering of the brethren; believing it to be wisdom to unite together as much as possible, in extending the hand of charity for the relief of the poor, who were suffering under the hand of persecution in Missouri; and to pursue that course that would prove for the general good of the whole church who was suffering for the gospel sake: and would advise the saints to settle (if possible) in companies, or in a situation so as to be organized into churches that they might be nourished and fed by the shepherds; for without, the sheep would be scattered. And he also impressed it upon the minds of the saints to give heed to the revelations of God especially the elders should be careful to depart from all iniquity, and to remember the council given by those whom God hath placed as councellors [councilors] in his church, that they may become as wise stewards in the vineyard of the Lord, that every man may know and act in his own place, for their is order in the kingdom of God, and we must regard that order if we expect to blessed.

Elder Young also stated that Elder Johnathan Dunham had received previous instructions not to call any conferences in this state, or elsewhere; but to go forth and preach repentance which was his calling, but contrary to those instructions he called a conference in Springfield, Ill. and presided there and brought forth the business which he had to transact, and his proceeding in many respects during the conference was contrary to the feelings of Elder W. Woodruff and other official members who were present; they considered his proceedings contrary to the will, and order of God. The conference then voted that Elder J. Dunham be reproved for his improper course, and that he be advised to adhere to the council given him. And after transacting various other business, Elder George W. Harris made some remarks relative to those who had left us in the times of our perils, persecution, and dangers and were acting against the interest of the church, and that the church could no longer hold them in fellowship unless they repented of their sins and turned unto God. After the conference fully expressed their feelings upon the subject, it was unanimously voted that the following persons be excommunicated from the church of Jesus Christ of Latter Day Saints, viz: George M. Hinckle, Sampson Avard, John Corrill, Reed Peck, Wm. W. Phelps, Frederick G. Williams, Thomas B. Marsh, Burr Riggs, and several others. After which the conference closed by prayer. BRIGHAM YOUNG, Pres't.

ROBERT B. THOMPSON, CLERK.

TO THE PATRONS OF THE TIMES & SEASONS

When we issued our prospectus for this paper we saw no good reason why we could not furnish them regularly each month as proposed, (as we were practical printers by profession,) but just as we got the first number in type and ready for the press, which was in July last we were taken severely ill with the chill fever, and were compelled to suspend our labor for the time, hoping that a few days, or weeks at most, would find us in possession of sufficient health to again resume our business; but in this we were sadly disappointed, for not only days and weeks passed, but months rolled away, and we still lingered upon our sick beds borne down under the raging influence of a burning fever. Had this been all our afflictions, we could have endured them with a good degree of fortitude, and would almost have considered them light; but not only ourselves, but our families also suffered with the same direful disease, and were brought nigh unto death; but through the tender mercies of a kind and benificent [beneficent] Providence, our lives are all spared, and our health sufficiently restored to enable us once more to resume our business.,

The above unavoidable circumstances, having compelled us to delay the publication of our paper until the present date, (notwithstanding we issued a few of this number in July,) have induced us to alter the date, to November, for the commencement of the volume; and we trust that hereafter we shall be enabled to furnish the paper to its patrons in due season.

+ Upon our twelfth page will be seen a communication from the Twelve, written in July, in which they informed us that they intended starting to England soon, upon a mission. They have left, some time since, accompanied by their beloved brother, Parley P. Pratt, who had been confined in prison nine months, in Missouri, for the truth's sake.

PROSPECTUS OF THE TIMES AND SEASONS.

The Subscribers being acquainted with the scattered condition of the church of Jesus Christ of Latter Day Saints, and realizing the anxiety which rests in the bosoms of all the Saints who are scattered abroad, to learn of the condition and welfare of the church, have procured a printing press and materials and will publish a monthly Periodical, at this place containing all general information respecting the church; as also, a history of the unparallelled [unparalleled] persecution, which we, as a people, received in Missouri by order of the Executive of that State-by which many innocent men and children were most inhumanly [inhumanely] murdered-others draged [dragged] from the bosom of their families, without any process whatever, by an armed soldiery, and thrust into prison and irons, there remaining for a long time without knowing the reason why they were thus treated-women insulted-houses plundered and burned-and finally, to end the scene of persecution, expell [expel], as exiles, from the State, in the winter season, the whole society; in all, from ten to *twelve thousand souls*! A statement of facts concerning the foregoing transactions, will not be uninteresting to all who wish to see the pure principles of Republicanism preserved unviolated.

The Times and Seasons will contain communications from the traveling Elders, from time to time: its columns will also, frequently be enriched with letters from gentlemen travelling [traveling] in Europe, which will greatly augment its interest.

It is not the intention of the Publishers, to admit any thing into this paper which will be calculated to engender strife or turmoil, neither will they interfere with political matters; as it is not their wish to cultivate any principle which tends to put people at variance one with another, but rather those principles that are calculated to make men happy in this world, and secure unto them eternal life in that which is to come.

TERMS: ONE DOLLAR per annum, payable, in all cases, in advance. Any person procuring 10 subscribers, and forwarding us ten dollars current money, shall receive one volume gratis. All current Bank notes, of any denomination will be received on subscriptions. Letters on business must be addressed to the Publishers, POST PAID. ROBINSON & SMITH.

Commerce, Hancock Co. Illinois, July, 1839.

TIMES AND SEASONS

"TRUTH WILL PREVAIL"

Vol. 1. Whole No. 2.] COMMERCE, ILLINOIS, DECEMBER 1839 [Whole No. 2.

A HISTORY, OF THE PERSECUTION, OF THE CHURCH OF JESUS CHRIST, OF LATTER DAY SAINTS IN MISSOURI.

In presenting to our readers, a history of the persecution of the church of Jesus Christ of Latter Day Saints, in the State of Missouri, we feel it our duty to commence it at the beginning. We are well aware, that many of our readers are well acquainted with the outrages, committed in Jackson county, (on account of their having been published in the Evening and Morning Star,) and might perhaps rather see the paper filled with other matter, than to have those former troubles presented before them again. Yet there are a great many others who are altogether unacquainted with those early persecutions, who would feel that we had not done our duty, were we to pass by them., and confine our history, to more recent transactions.

In the winter of 1830-31, five elders of the church of Jesus Christ, travelled [traveled] through the prairies in a deep snow,(which is not common in that country,) from St. Louis to Jackson county Missouri, where they made a permanent stand. They preached about the country as the way opened before them.-A few believed the gospel which they preached, and had been baptized, when about the middle of the following July, a number more arrived at the same place: Shortly afterwards a small branch of the church arrived there also. At that time there appeared to be but little objection to our people settling there; notwithstanding some, who could not endure the truth, manifested hostile feelings.

The church in Jackson continued to increase, almost constantly, until it was driven from the county.

As the church increased the hostile spirit of the people increased also.-The enemies of false stories against the saints, hoping thereby to stir up the indignation of others. In the spring of 1832 they began to brick-bat or stone the houses of the saints, breaking in windows, &c., not only disturbing, but endangering the lives of the inmates. In the course of that season a county meeting was called at Independence, to adopt measures, to drive our people from the country; but the meeting broke up, without coming to any agreement about them; having had too much confusion among themselves, to do more than to have a few knock-downs, after taking a plentiful supply of whisky. The result of this meeting may be attributed in part, to the influence of certain patriotic individuals; among whom General Clark, a sub-Indian agent, may be considered as principal, He hearing of the meeting, came from his agency, or from home, some thirty of forty miles distant, a day or two before the meeting.

He appeared quite indignant, at the idea of having the constitution and laws set at defiance, and trodden under foot, by the many trampling upon the rights of the few. He went to certain influencial mob characters, and offered to decide the case with them in single combat: he said that it would be better for one or two individuals to die, than for hundreds to be put to death.

Although the meeting broke up without being able to effect a union, still the hostile spirit of individuals was no less abated: such was their thirst for the destruction of the saints, that they, that same fall, shot into the houses of certain individuals. On ball in particular lodged in a log near the head of the owner of the house, as he lay in bed.

During the winter and spring of 1833, the mob spirit spread itself, though in a manner secretly; but in the forepart of the summer it began to show itself openly, in the stoning of houses and other insults. Sometime in July the unparalleled declaration of the people of Jackson county, made its appearance; in which they appear to have tried their utmost, to defame our people, charging them with crimes, and many other things; at the same time acknowledging that the laws of the land would not reach the case of the Mormons: which was evidently a fact, for they hold the reins of government in their own hands, or in other words, had the administering of the laws themselves; and could they have found the laws broken, even in a single instance, who does not know, that they would have put it in force? and thereby substantiated their charges against the saints, which they never did do, in preference to taking unlawful measures against them.

The following remarkable sentence, is near the close of their famous declaration. "We therefore agree, that after timely warning., and receiving an adequate compensation for what little property they," [the Mormons,] "cannot take with them, they refuse to leave us in peace, as they found us, we agree to use such means as may be sufficient to remove them; and to that end we each pledge to each other, our bodily powers, our lives, fortunes, and sacred honors." The 20th of July was the day set, for the people to come together, and commence their work of destruction Accordingly they met to the number of from 3 to 500. A committee of 13 of the mob, requested an interview with some of the principal elders of the church: Six were soon called together, who met the mob committee. They demanded of those elders, to have the printing office, and indeed all other mechanic shops, belonging to our people, together with Gilbert & Whitney's store, closed forthwith; and the society to leave the county immediately. Those elders asked for three months, to consider upon their demand, which was refused, they then asked for ten days, when they were informed that fifteen minutes were the most that could be granted. Being driven to the necessity of giving an immediate answer, and being interrogated seperately, they each one answered that they could not consent to their demands: upon which one of the mob observed, as he left the room, that he was sorry, for, said he, the work of destruction will commence immediately. In a short time, hundreds of the mob gathered around the printing office, (which was a, two story brick building,) which they soon threw down. The press was thrown from the upper story, and the aparatus, book work, paper, type, &c., &c., scattered through the streets. A family, residing in the lower story, was also thrust out in great haste. After destroying the printing establishment, they proceeded to Gilbert & Whitney's store for the same purpose, but Gilbert agreeing to shut it, and box the goods soon, they concluded to let it alone.-They then went in search of certain individuals, for the purpose of taking, and abusing them. They succeeded in taking Edward Patridge, and Charles Allen, both of whom they tarred and feathered, upon the public square, surrounded by hundreds of the mob.-A number more were taken, but they succeeded in making their escape, through the over anxiety of their keepers, who wished to have the sport of seeing those who were being tarred.-This scene ended the work of the mob for that day; and they adjourned to meet the next Tuesday, the 23d inst.

On Tuesday morning, large companies of the mob rode into Independence bearing red flags, threatening death and destruction, to the Mormons. A consultation was held by some of the leading men of both parties. Nothing appeared satisfactory to the mob but for our people to either leave the county or be put to death. Seeing the determination of the mob, some few of the leading elders offered their lives, provided that would satisfy them, so as to let the rest of the society live, where they then lived, in peace; they would not agree to this, but said that every one should die for themselves, or leave the county. At that time, the most, if not all, of our people, in Jackson, thought they would be doing wrong, to resist the mob, even by defending themselves; consequently they thought, that they must quietly submit, to whatever yoke was put upon them, even to the laying down of theirs lives.

With these views, the few elders who were assembled, at the time, to consult up the subject, (which were but six or seven,) after counselling [counseling] what time they had, thought it best to agree to leave the county, upon the terms agreed upon, viz: that those elders should go themselves, and also use their influence, with the society, to have one half of them leave the county by the first of January, and the other half by the first of April, 1834; hoping that before either of those dates would expire, providence would kindly open the way for them, to still live there in peace. The mob party agreed to not molest the saints, during the time agreed upon for them to stay. The agreement was written, and signed by the parties; the whole mob was then assembled in the court-house, and had it read, and explained to them by their leaders; they all appeared satisfied, and agreed to abide by it. The saints were not pleased with the idea of leaving the county; and few of them, at first, believed that they would have to leave it, thinking that the government would protect them, in their constitutional rights. Threats of destruction were soon thrown out, by some of the mobbers, should they, [the saints] make any effort to get assistance from any quarter: but notwithstanding their threats a petition was carefully circulated, and obtained the signature of many of the saints; and was carried to the Governor of the State, before it become at all public. The petition set forth, in a concise manner, their persecutions; and solicited the aid of the Governor in protecting them, in their rights, that they might sue, and obtain damages, for loss of property, abuse, defamation, &c. The Governor, in his answer, expressed a willingness to help, but said he had no authority to do it, until the law could not be executed without force. He advised them to try the law, against those who should threaten their lives; and if the law was resisted, give him authentic information of the fact, and then he would see that it was enforced. He also advised them to sue for their damages. They accordingly employed four counsellors [counselors], at $1,000 to commence and carry their suits, more or less, through to final judgment.

About that time a few families moved into Van Buren county, the county south of Jackson; but the hostile spirit of the inhabitants, which was manifested by their threatnings; induced them to move back again to Jackson.

The saints, as yet, had made no resistance, but seeing; as they thought, the only feasible door for moving away shut against them, they began to look around, to see what could be done.-They took the subject of self defence [defense] into consideration, and they found that they would be justified by the laws of both God man, in defending themselves, their families and houses, against all such as should molest them unlawfully, They therefore concluded, that from that time forward, they would defend themselves, as well as they could, against mobbers; hoping that that, when it should be understood, would dampen the hostile spirit of those who were, at that time, continually threatening them. But it had a contra effect. That, together with the petitioning of the Governor, and the employing of counsel, caused the mob to rage again; They began by stoning houses, breaking in windows and doors, and committing other outrages; but nothing, very serious, was done till the last of October. On Thursday night the 31st, a mob of forty or fifty, collected and proceeded armed to a branch of the church, wuo [who] lived eight or ten miles, south west of Independence; there they unroofed ten houses, and partly threw down the bodies of some of them; they caught three or four of the men, and notwithstanding the cries, and entreaties of their wives and children, they whiped [whipped], and beat them in a barbarous manner. Others evaded a beating by flight. They were taken by surprise by the mob, consequently were not collected together, or in a situation to defend themselves against so large a body; therefore they made no resistance. The mob, after threatening to visit them again in a rougher manner, dispersed. The news of this outrage soon spread through the different settlements of the saints, and produced feelings more easily felt than described; for the very well knew by the threatnings of the mob, and their breaking the treaty, or agreement, which was made but a few days before, as it were, that there was trouble ahead. They were in a scattered situation, their settlements extending east and was ten or twelve miles, and what to do for their safety, they knew not. To resist large bodies of the mob, in their scattered situation, appeared useless; and to gather together into one body, immediately, was impracticable, for they had not in any one place, houses to dwell in, or food for themselves and stock. A consultation was held, near Independence, by some of the principal men of the church, to see what was best to be done; it was concluded to obtain peace warrants, if possible, against some of the principal leaders, of the mob; and also to advise their brethren to gather together, into four or five bodies, in their different neighborhoods, and defend themselves, as well as they could, whenever the mob should come upon them. They then went to a magistrate, and applied for a warrant, but he refused to grant one.

The Governor's letter, directing them to proceed in that way, was then read to him, upon which he replied that he cared nothing about it. At that very time the streets were filled with mobbers, passing and repassing, threatening the saints, in different directions, with destruction. And to be deprived of the benefit of law, at such a critical time, was well calculated to make the saints feel solemn, and mourn over the depravity of man. But they had not much time for reflection; for they had many things to do to prepare for the night, which was just at hand, in the which they expected the mob would be upon them. Up to this time, the persons of women and children were considered safe, they seldom being abused; therefore the men run together for the night, leaving their families at home.

At Independence the men met half a mile west of the Court house.-Night came on and a party of the mob, who had staid in the village, were heard brick-batting the houses; spies were sent to discover their movements, who returned with information that they were tearing down a brick-house, belonging to Gilbert and Whitney, and also breaking open their store. Upon hearing that news, those who were collected together, formed themselves into two small companies, and marched up to the public square where they found a number of men in the act of stoning the store of Gilbert and Whitney,(which was broken open, and some of the goods thrown into the street) they all fled but one Richard McCarty, who was taken and found to be well lined with whiskey. Gilbert and one or two more went with him to Esq. Westons, and demanded a warrant for him, but he refused to give them one; consequently McCarty was liberated. Next morning it was ascertained that the windows were broken in, where there were none but women and children; one house in particular, which had window shutters, and they were shut, had a rail thrust through into the room where women and children were alone. Seeing that neither sex nor age were safe, the families were all moved out of the village that day. The same night another party of the mob collected about ten or twelve miles from Independence, near a body of the saints; two of their company went to discover the situation of the brethren; they cane near the guard, when P. P. Pratt discovering them, advanced and went up to them:

when one of them struck him over the head with a rifle, which cut a large gash in his head, and nearly knocked him down; but he recovered himself, called to his men who were near, they took the spies and disarmed them of two rifles and three pistols, kept them in custody until morning, then gave them their arms and let them go without injuring them. The rest of their company were heard at a distance, but they dispersed without doing any harm. TO BE CONTINUED

COMMUNICATIONS.

To the Saints scattered abroad, GREETING:

Having given my testimony to the world of the truth of the book of Mormon, the renewal of the everlasting covenant, and the establishment of the Kingdom of heaven, in these last days; and having been brought into great afflictions and distresses for the same, I thought that it might be strengthening to my beloved brethren, to give them a short account of my sufferings, for the truth's sake, and the state of my mind and feelings, while under circumstances of the most trying and afflicting nature, It would be unnecessary for me to enter into the particulars, prior to my settlement in Missouri, or give an account of my journey to that State; suffice it to say, that after having endured almost all manner of abuse, which was poured out upon the church of Latter Day Saints, from its commencement, by wicked and ungodly men; I left Kirtland, Ohio, the beginning of March 1838, with a family consisting of ten individuals, and with means only sufficient to take us one half the way; the weather was very unpropitious, and the roads were worse than I had ever seen them before. However, after enduring many privations and much fatigue, through the kind providence of God, I arrived with my family in Far West, the latter part of May. where I found many of my friends who had borne the heat and burthen [burden] of the day, and whose privations and sufferings for Christ's sake had been great, with whom I fondly hoped, and anticipated the pleasure of spending a season in peace, and have a cessation from the troubles and persecutions to which we had been subject for a number of years, the prospect was truly flattering, we were the owners, of almost the entire county; many of the brethren had already opened very extensive farms; nature was propitious, and the comforts of life would have soon been realized by every industrious person But notwithstanding these favorable auspices, a storm arose before whose withering blast our fair and reasonable prospects were blasted, and ruined; anarchy, and dismay, was spread through that county, as well as the adjoining ones, in which our brethren had found a resting place.

The inhabitants of the upper counties, jealous of the increasing number of the saints, thinking like some in ancient times, that if they were to let us alone we should take away their place and nation, soon began to circulate reports prejudicial to the saints, and after threatening us with mobs for some time, at last put their threats into execution, & proceeded to drive off our cattle, and burn down our houses, while helpless females with their tender offsprings, had to flee into the wilderness, and wander to a considerable distance for shelter; this state of things continued until, from false representations, and a wicked desire to overthrow the saints, the Governor called out the militia, and gave orders for our extermination.

Soon after the arrival of the militia at Far West, my brother Joseph, with several others, who were considered leading characters in the church, were betrayed into their hands, and the day after Colonel George Hinckle, who had always been a professed friend, but who had now turned traitor, came with a company of the enemy to my house, and told them I was the person whom they sought; ;they told me I must go with them to the camp.-I inquired when I could return, my family being in a situation, that I knew not how to leave them, but could get no answer, remonstrance was in vain, so I was obliged to go with them. I was aware of the hostile feelings of our enemies, and their hatred to all those who professed the faith of the church of Latter Day Saints; and I can assure my brethren, that I would as soon have gone into a den of Lions, as into that host, who had orders from the Executive of the state to put us to death, and who had every disposition to do so; however, I was enabled to put my trust in the Lord, knowing that he who delivered Daniel out of the den of lions, could deliver me from cruel and wicked men. When I arrived at the camp, I was put under the same guard with my Brother Joseph and my other friends, who had been taken the day previous.

That evening a court martial was held to consult what steps should be taken with the prisoners, when it was decided that we were to be shot the next morning, as an ensample to the rest of the church. Knowing that I had done nothing worthy of "death or of bonds," and feeling an assurance that all things would work together for our good. I remained quite calm, and felt altogether unmoved, when I heard of their unjust and cruel sentence "my heart was fixed, trusting in the Lord."

The next morning came on, when (according to the sentence of the court) we were to be shot. It was an important time, thousands were anticipating the event with fiendish joy, and seemed to long for the hour of execution, while our friends and brethren, were beseeching a throne of grace on our behalf, and praying for our deliverance. The time at length arrived when their sentence was to be carried into effect, but in consequence of General Doniphan protesting against the unlawfulness of the proceedings, and at the same time, threatning [threatening] to withdraw his troops, if they should offer to carry into effect their murderous sentence, the court resigned their resolution, and thus their purposes were frustrated and our bitterest enemies were disappointed; the prayers of our friends were answered, and our lives spared. Notwithstanding the discomfiture of their plans, yet our distruction [destruction] was determined upon by a vast majority, who, thinking they could better carry into effect their purposes, ordered us to be conveyed to Jackson county, where they were well aware our most cruel persecutors resided.-Before starting I got permission to visit my family, but had only time to get a change of clothes, and then was hurried away from them, while they clung to my garments; they supposing it would be the last time they would see me in this world. While getting into the waggon [wagon] which was to convey us to our destination, four men rushed upon us, and leveled their rifles at us, seemingly, with a determination to shoot us, but this was not

49

permitted them to do, no, their arms were unnerved, and they droped [dropped] their pieces and slunk away. While thus exposed I felt no tremour [tremor] or alarm, I knew I was in the hands of God, whose power was unlimited.

While on our way to Jackson county we excited great curiosity; at our stoping [stopping] places, people would flock to see us, from all quarters; a great number of whom would rail upon us, and give us abusive language, while a few would pity us; knowing that we were an injured people. When we arrived at Independence, the county seat of Jackson County, the citizens flocked from all parts of the county to see us, they were generally very abusive some of the most ignorant gnashed their teeth upon us: but all their threats and abuse did not move me, for I felt the spirit of the Lord to rest down upon me, and I felt great liberty in speaking to those who would listen to the truth.

Notwithstanding the determination of our enemies, they were not suffered to carry out their designs in that county, for after enduring considerable hardships, we were removed back as far as Richmond in Ray county, where for the first time in my life I was put into prison and my feet hurt with fetters: and remained in this situation for fourteen days. I endeavored to bear up under my sufferings and wrongs, but at the same time could not help but feel indignant at those who treated us with such cruelty, and who pretended to do it under the sanction of the laws. After many attempts to destroy us by the military, in all of which they were unsuccessful, we were at length delivered up to the civil law: soon after which a court of inquiry was held; a great deal of false testimony was given prejudicial to my brethren, but all the testimony they could produce against me was, that I was one of the Presidency of the church, and a firm friend to my brother Joseph. This the court deemed sufficient to authorize my committal to prison; I was then, with my brethren, removed to Liberty, in Clay county, where I was confined for more than four months, and suffered much for want of proper food, and from the nauseous cell in which I was confined: but still more so on account of my anxiety for my family, whom I had left without any protector, and who were unable to help themselves; my wife was confined while I was away from home, and had to suffer more than tongue can tell; she was not able to sit up for several weeks, and heigthen [heighten] my affliction, and the sufferings of my helpless family, my goods were unlawfully seized upon and carried off, until my family had to suffer in consequence thereof: nor, were the Missourians my only oppressors, but those with whom I had been acquainted from my youth, and who had ever pretended the greatest friendship towards me, came to my house while I was in prison, and ransacked and carried off many of my valuables, this they did under the cloak of friendship. Amongst those who treated me thus I cannot help making particular mention of Lyman Cowdery, who, in connexion [connection] with his brother Oliver, took from me a great many things; and to cap the climax of his iniquity, compelled my aged father, by threatning [threatening] to bring a mob upon him to deed over to him, or his brother Oliver, about 160 acres of land to pay a note which he said I had given to Oliver for $165, such a note I confess I was, and still am entirely ignorant of, and after mature consideration, I have to say that I believed it must be a forgery.

These circumstances, with the afflicting situation of my family, served greatly to heighten my grief; indeed it was almost more than I could bear up under; I traversed my prison house for hours, thinking of their cruelty to my family, and the afflictions they brought upon the saints of the Most High; they forcibly reminded me of the children of Edom, when the Jews were destroyed by their enemies, and the language of prophet Obadiah to Edom, is, I think, so very much in point that I cannot refrain from inserting it.

"For thy violence against thy brother Jacob, shame shall cover thee and thou shalt be cut off forever.

In the day thou stoodest on the other side, in the day that the strangers carried away captive his forces, and foreigners entered into his gates, and cast lots upon Jerusalem even thou wast as one of them.

But thou shouldest not have looked on the day of thy brother in the day hat he became a stranger; neither shoudst thou have rejoiced over the children of Judah in the day of their destruction; neither shouldst thou have spoken proudly in the day of distress.

Thou shouldst not have entered into the gate of my people in the day of their calamity; yea, thou shoudst not have looked on their affliction in the day of their calamity, nor have laid hands on their substance in the day of their calamity. Neither shouldst thou have stood in the crossways, to cut off those of his that did escape; neither shouldst thou have delivered up those of his that did remain in the day of distress."

After being in the hands of our enemies for about six months, the time of our deliverance at length arrived, as mentioned by my brother Joseph, in the last number of the "Times and Seasons." You may judge what my feelings were when I escaped from those whose feet were fast to shed blood, and when I was again priviledged [privileged] to see my beloved family who had suffered so many privations and afflictions; not only while in Far West, but likewise in moving away in that inclement season of the year. Thus I have endeavored to give you a short account of my sufferings while in the state of Missouri, but how inadequate is language to express the feelings of my mind, while under them: knowing that I was innocent of crime, and that I had been dragged from my family at a time, when my assistance was most needed; that I had been abused and thrust into a dungeon, and confined for months on account of my faith, and the "testimony of Jesus Christ." However I thank God that I felt a determination to die, rather than deny the things which my eyes had seen, which my hands had handled, and which I hard borne testimony to, wherever my lot had been cast; and I can assure my beloved brethren that I was enabled to bear as strong a testimony, when nothing but death presented itself, as ever I did in my life. My confidence in God, was likewise unshaken. I knew that he who suffered me along with my brethren, to be thus tried, that he could and that he would deliver us out of the hands of our enemies; and in his own due time he did so, for which I desire to bless and praise his holy name.

From my close and long confinement, as well as from the sufferings of my mind, I feel my body greatly broke down and debilitated, my frame has received a shock from which it will take a long time to recover; yet, I am happy to say that my zeal for the cause of God, and my courage in defence [defense] of the truth, are as great as ever. "My heart is fixed," and I yet feel a determination to do the will of God, in spite of persecutions, imprisonments or death; I can say with Paul "none of these things move me, so that I may finish my course with joy."

Dear Brethren we have nothing to be discouraged at, if we remember the words of the Savior, which say "in the world you shall have tribulation.-If they have persecuted me they will also persecute you." The world has always hated the truth and those who have testified of the same; let us not then think that these are strange things which has never happened before, but, rather let us take the prophets and saints in ancient days as ensamples.

To those who have suffered bereavements in consequence of the cruelties of the wicked, whose husbands, fathers, &c. have been slain, with you, I would drop the sympathetic tear, and would do all I could to comfort you in your distress, and would fain pour into your wounded souls, the oil of joy for mourning; the time is fast hastening, when if faithful, you will join your friends in a more glorified state of existance [existence], where mobs and oppression are not known: look then at the things which are before, and not at those which are behind.

To the church in general I would say, be faithful, maintain your integrity, let the principles of truth and righteousness get deep hold in your hearts, live up to those principles at all times, be humble withall, and then you will be able to stand firm and unshaken tho'

> "The mountains skip like rams, And all the little hills like lambs."

Your Brother,

n the Kingdom and patience of Jesus Christ.

HYRUM SMITH.

Commerce, Dec. 1839.

KEOKUK

LEE

LEE COUNTY, IOWA TERRITORY.

This placed is situated on the west bank of the Mississippi River, about forty miles above Quincy, Illinois, at the foot of the Rapids, which is the first obstruction to the navigation for the largest class of Steam Boats.-At this place all Steam Boats, in ascending the Mississippi at low water, are compelled to discharge their cargoes, which are transported over the Rapids in lighters, and on descending, the boats receive their cargoes from the lighters at this place. The landing is equal to any on the River. And no part of the town is ever overflowed.

A part of this place has recently been purchased by the Bishop of the Church of Latter Day Saints. Bishop Knight has also purchased another town six miles above Keokuk, which is called Nashville, it being at the head of the Rapids, the place has advantages equal to any town on the Mississippi; it has a large body of valuable timber attached to it, and the surrounding country is beautifully interspersed with prairies which will admit of a dense population: these advantages together with the advantage of landing, renders the country valuable.

MONTROSE:-This place is four miles above Nashville, it is situated on a bottom prairie, and a handsome place for a town, it has equal advantages with other town on Mississippi. Bishop Knight has also, purchased a part of this town, together with about thirty thousand acres of the surrounding country, on the point of land between the Mississippi and the Desmoine, generally denominated the Half Breed tract; this tract has actually superior advantages, having the Desmoine on the West, and the Mississippi on the East, both navigable streams; and the soil is generally acknowledged to be nearly equal to that of the State of Missouri. The Half Breed tract contains 119,000 acres, and the whole tract can be purchased by a united effort of the saints.

NAUVOO.-This is a newly located Town, and is situated on the East bank of the Mississippi opposite Montrose, it derived its name from the Hebrew, which signifies Fair, very beautiful, and it actually fills the definition of the word; for nature has not formed a parallel on the Banks of the Mississippi, from New Orleans to Galena, for the beauty of the ground on which it stands; there is a good landing and it has equal privileges with other towns, this is also owned by the saints, and is rapidly increasing; the surrounding country is fertile, and the crops, this present year, are good, therefore there is no fear existing that the gathering will be too extensive.

A. RIPLY.

TIMES AND SEASONS

COMMERCE, ILL. DEC. 1839.

We are favored with several communications from traveling Elders, who, in almost every instance, make the Macedonian call, "come over and help us;" as they have more calls for preaching than they can possibly fill. Also, great inquires are made for Books of all kinds, which have been published in the church, and as they are all disposed of, and not a copy, of scarce a single work now to be obtained, therefore the Presidency and high council of this place, having taken the subject into consideration, passed the following resolution:

"*Resolved*, That Ten thousand copies of a Hymn Book, be printed; also that the Book of Mormon be re-printed in this place, under the inspection of the Presidency, as soon as monies [moneys] can be raised to defray the expenses."

FROM THE ELDERS ABROAD

Elder Henry Dean, writes from Lancaster county, Pa. under date of Sept. 30th 1839. After giving a suscinct [succinct] account of his travels and labours [labors] through different parts of Pennsylvania, he says: I am now in Lancaster county, near Strasbury, in company with brother Davis, we are raising a church in this place, and we expect it will be a middling large Branch: there are 3 baptized, and 5 or 6 more to be baptized to day, and a good number more in this place believing; and I can say, the work is gaining ground in these parts, though the labourers [laborers] are few. The work is prospering every where the elders have been. We desire an interest in your prayers, that we may pull down priest-craft in this place, and raise the standard of truth in its stead.

Brother A. Petty writes, from Dover, Stuart county, Tennessee, in which he informs us, that the work of the Lord is still rolling on in the south: "Some few are still coming into the church in this country, brother Brandon has lately baptized four, and he thinks there is a prospect of more."

Brother Nathaniel Holmes, writes from Georgetown Mass. dated October 11th 1839, by way of encouragement to the Saints, he says: we would say to the brethren in that place, we feel anxious for your prosperity, the few members of the little church remaining in Georgetown and vicinity, are firm in the doctrine of the gospel revealed in these last days, and I trust will out-ride the storm of persecution; from the signs in the heavens, and on the earth, we look for the fulfilling of the ancient prophets, apostles, and Jesus himself, on this generation.

Elder G. H. Brandon, writes from Benton county, Tennessee, under date of Sept. 3d 1839. He states that the work of God is going on in that place, the honest in heart are still embracing the truth in Benton county, he has baptized 5 and organized a branch of the church called the charity branch, consisting of 8 members: he also says; "The people seem to be much inquiring. I have more calls for preaching that I can fill; the enemy is raging on every hand, yet the work seems to be spreading very fast at present, insomuch [inasmuch] , that where I had calls last fall and winter, I now have so many that I cannot fill them all; where I had no bounds, they have become so large, that I am called as mush as 25 miles from home in different directions. We would take it as a great blessing if some of the Elders would visit us this fall."

Elder James Blakeslee writes from Waterville, Oneida co. N. Y. under date of July 22nd, in the following language.

Since last fall, through the goodness and mercies of our God, I have been enabled to organize two branches of the Church of Jesus Christ of Latter Day Saints, consisting of about sixty members; one in Boonville, Oneida county, and the other in Williamstown, and Amboy, Oswego county N. Y., and I have baptized between twenty and thirty in this region, within about one month; there are many believeing [believing] in this north country, notwithstanding the troubles which have befallen the saints in the west, in their great persecution; yet the work of our God rolls forth in mighty power, being propelled by the power of Israel's God. The saints in this country are growing stronger and stronger, of late, and are very anxious to remove and suffer with their brethren in Zion, and the probability is, (nothing in providence forbiding [forbidding]],) a large company will remove west next season. We were very happy to hear from our beloved brother Joseph Smith jr. and others, and that they were restored to the sweet society of their families, and brethren in Christ: they have had the prayers of the saints in their behalf, for their deliverance in this region, ever since we first heard of their being confined in prison; and we have great reason to praise the Lord, that he has thus far granted our petition in relieving our beloved brethren from the prison; and our sincere prayer to God, is, that he would set at liberty the rest of our beloved brethren, who are still in confinement, and we will ever pray and praise his holy name.

Elder B. Winchester writes from Philadelphia, Pa. under date of Oct. 21st. from which we learn that he has introduced the gospel into that city with good success; many are embracing the truth; he solicits *help* on the *strongest* terms; some faithful elder would be doing their Masters business, if they would call and lend him assistance.

Thus the work of God continues a steady and unimpeded course, and though its progress is slow, yet it will continue to roll forth, until the honest in heart are gathered out, and Israel "hunted from every mountain, and from every high hill, and out of the holes of the rocks;" and nothing can hinder it in its decreed course; although the threshing flail of Missouri, with the combined powers of hell, has pounced heavily upon the church of God, yet, (like striking the mustard stalk when ripe,) it has only served to scatter the seed, (the word) throughout, not only the small Garden of the United States, but across the mighty ocean, among foreign nations; and it will continue to spring up, and grow, and bear fruit, until the bursting heavens shall reveal the Son of God, and that to the final consumation [consummation] of all those "that know not God, and that obey not the gospel of our Lord Jesus Christ," when the church of the Most High, who have been persecuted, smitten and afflicted for the testimony of Jesus Christ, yea, even those who love his appearing, unto them shall he appear the second time, without sin unto salvation, and that to the joy of their hearts.

Pleasant Garden, Putnam co. Indiana.

October, 18 1839

TO D. C. SMITH, E. ROBINSON:

Dear Brethren,

In great haste I improve this opportunity of addressing a few lines to you, to inform you where I am laboring, and the fruits that attend the same. I left Springfield on the third of September, for the East, more particular to visit my friends, and consequently took my wife along, we traveled about 80 miles from Springfield, and my horse was taken sick and I was obliged to stop; I went to preaching for one week, baptized five; I continued my journey on East, crossed the Wabash river at Terre-Haute, continued on twenty five miles and stoped [stopped] in Plesent Garden, to take supper; the people found out that I was a Mormon, and they wanted me to stop and preach the same evening, which I did; but the people were not content and wanted I should preach the next evening, which I did;

after I had preached the second time the people began to cry out that the Mormons were not driven from Missouri, for preaching such doctrine as that, but in order to prove their own statement false, on the third evening, after meeting they took my carriage and drawed it about one mile into the woods, broke it very badly; they also took off one of the wheels, and carried it off, and I have never heard from it since: however, I have got a new one made, and the people made a collection and paid for it, and of course while I was getting my waggon [wagon] repaired, I kept preaching to the people, which I did for seven nights in succession; then the people began to invite me into other places, I was invited to go to Green Castle and preach in the court house, which I have done five times, without being disturbed but once, and the man that disturbed me was fined five dollars. I have held 33 meetings here, and have calls, more than I can possibly attend; prejudice is giving away on all sides, I have just began to baptize here, I have baptized five, among whom is Doctor Knights and Lady, an eminent physician, who has practiced in this country for 13 years. The prospect is that many of the first class of people in the county will be baptized, I have been in this church eight years, in which you know I have travelled [traveled] much, and I can say, that never has a greater field opened than I am in now, and I want help immediately; I want an elder of experience sent here as soon as you receive this, why I say an elder of experience, is because here is the seat of literature for this State, here are 80 collegians, and professors and priests without number. I have had 3 attacks from them, but have found that they could do nothing against the truth, but for it.

Yours in the bond of the everlasting covenant. ALMON BABBIT.

Wilmington, Del. Sept. 8th, 1839.

Elder D. C. SMITH:

Highly esteemed brother in Christ, and fellow laborer in the Kingdom of our God set up for the last time, and to all saints, GREETING:

Though mobs may rise and Satan may rage and stir up his emissaries against the work of God in the Last Days; yet they cannot overthrow it. As well might they try to stop the sun in its course through the heavens, or prevent its shining upon the earth beneath, as to try to stop the spread of truth. The honest in heart will hear and will understand, and obey.-And I am thoroughly convinced, there never has been a better time for the elders of the Church of Latter Day Saints, to preach the fullness of the gospel to the world than at the present time. After elder Sagers and myself had visited the saints in Virginia and Ohio, (and accomplished our business with as far as circumstances would permit,) E. D. Woolly, and Elisha H. Davis, started for the eastern countries, crossed the Alleghany mountains in the cold month of January, proclaiming the everlasting gospel whenever an opportunity was presented; visited the saints in Bedford co. and after a journey of four weeks, arrived in Chester co. Pa. Here we planted the standard of truth among Elder Woolly's friends and acquaintances; doors were open on the right and left, and in a very short time whole neighborhoods were in an uproar, on account of the strange doctrine as they called it, which had come to their ears. Mormonism, as it was termed, was the principle subject of discussion. The dust was brushed from many a bible which I presume had lain useless for years, and a general search of the scriptures was made, so that it was said, and I think in truth, the bible was read more by the people in a few weeks after we arrived in the place, than it had been before for many years. Indeed, a certain doctor acknowledged in public that he had read the bible more within 3 days than he had in 15 years before-Soon after arriving in the co. Elder Woolly and myself visited West Chester, the county seat, a town containing about 2,000 inhabitants, and held several meetings in the old fellows' hall. The Methodist became very much alarmed, supposing, no doubt, that their craft was in danger, (for the people were very attentive to hear,) and sent off immediately to the City of Philadelphia for a champion of theirs, by the name of Mattack, to come and put down the truth. But lo! when he came and got up to speak the people hissed at him . I tried to get him to appoint some time and we would meet and have a public discussion, but he refused, saying he must go to Philadelphia the next day. But instead of that, he went into the Methodist Chapel in the evening and read LeRoy Sundehladn's pamphlet. I attended, and when he was through I arose and read Parley P. Pratt's reply, but when I came to Methodism unveiled, the stationed preacher in the town arose and objected to my reading it, he however was overruled by the congregation, and I proceeded and read it off to the whole assembly, and sat down. Their champion Mr. Mattack made no reply; but the stationed preacher arose and said, (in a very sarcastic manner,) well if you wish to be Mormons, you may I have nothing to say, you are soon dismissed.

After this I understood, several of their members withdrew, or were turned out of their Church,. because they believed Mormonism.

We continued our preaching in different places through the county for several weeks when 4 came forward and obeyed the gospel; Elder Wooly then left us for his family in Ohio, Elder Sagers and myself shortly afterwards visited the City of Philadelphia, where we preached three times, and then visited the churches in N. Jersey, and N. Y. and after preaching a number of times in different places, returned; Elder Sagers then returned to his family in the West, and I resumed my labours [labors] in Chester county Pa. in company with Elder E. H. Davis. We have extended our labours [labors] to Lancaster county, and the northern part of the state of Delaware. The prospect is good in all these places; one has already obeyed the Gospel in Lancaster county, and many more are believing.

The church in Chester county, now number 30 members, and many more are believing, whom I trust will obey the gospel soon. The Lord has commenced a great and good work among this people, and I feel strong in the spirit, and am determined to thrust in my sickle, and reap, while the harvest lasts so that when we return, we may return laden with sheaves, pray for us dear brother, and may the Lord help us all, Amen.

Yours, in the bond, of the new and everlasting covenant.
LORENZO BARNES

Monmouth Co. N. J. Sept. 10th 1839 D. C. Smith and E. Robinson. Dear Brethren,

This morning having a few moments, I lift my pen to communicate the particulars of the woods meeting, which I mentioned in my last. The meeting commenced according to appointment on the 28th; was opened by singing, prayer and preaching by Jonathan Dunham; the congregation was serious and attentive. Thursday morning the meeting was addressed by B. Oliver Granger. During intermission the members of the conference retired; (who remained organized as at the previous conference,) Brother Granger's mission was presented for consideration.

The congregation assembled in the afternoon, and was addressed by Br. Green. The same serious attention was manifested during the day. Friday it rained, Saturday the congregation increased and was addressed by Brother Lorenzo Barnes. The members of the conference again retired for deliberation. It was moved, seconded, and a unanimous vote that Br. Benjamin Winchester go and preach in Philadelphia; Samuel James preside over the Church in N. J. Lorenzo Barnes preside over the Church in Chester Co. Pa. and Elisha H. Davis assist him, & J. Huston preach in Bucks co. Pa. In the afternoon the meeting was addressed by Brs. Winchester and Davis. This day deep interest was manifested in the congregation, and two presented themselves for baptism. Sunday they were baptised [baptized]. A large congregation, of from two to three thousand assembled, and were addressed in the morning by Br. Green and Br. Granger. In the afternoon Br. Green gave a relation of the persecution, and sufferings of the Brethren in Missouri. After which, a collection of $30 was lifted for them.

Monday, the Elders gave their testimony concerning the coming forth of the Book of Mormon, and their experimental knowledge of the work of God in these days. Br. Granger occupied the fore part of the day, and gave a very interesting account of his life; of the administration of angels, who testified of the work of God in the world; a vision of the Book of Mormon, the means by which he was brought into the church, and then bore testimony to the restoration of the Priesthood, and exhorted the people to embrace the truth, that they might be saved in the kingdom of God.

The people listened with attention; the tears of many, and the deep anxiety manifested, bespoke the impressions making on many hearts. In the afternoon Br. Barnes, Br. Winchester, Br. Dunham and Br. Green, testified to the truth of the work, which they had received by seeing, hearing, and experimental knowledge; such as visions, prophecies, revelations, healing etc. The same state of feelings continued in the congregation, while the spirit of God rested down upon some with mighty power, Truly it was a solemn and interesting time. Tuesday a large congregation assembled, Samuel James addressed them. In the afternoon he gave the testimony he had received of the truth of the work, exhorted the people, gave an invitation for baptism, assembled at the water and baptized eight; made several appointments, at some of which there are others to be baptized; these appointments have been fulfilled and six more were baptized; and last Sunday fourteen were confirmed, while solemnity, and seriousness pervaded the congregation. Thus truth prevails; the power of the spirit attends the preaching the word; conviction takes possession of the heart and leads its subjects to the door, and entering in, they are made to rejoice in the Holy One of Israel. May the Lord carry on his work until the nations have heard, the saints gathered home, the earth claensed [cleansed], and the kingdom established for ever. Brethren let us be up and doing, the time is short, and the kingdom is at hand. JOHN P. GREEN, PRES'T. SAMUEL JAMES, Clerk.

Commerce November, 1839

To the Saints scattered abroad, in the region westward from Kirtland Ohio.

Beloved Brethren, feeling that it is our duty, as the servants of God, to instruct the saints from time to time, in those things which to us appear to be wise and proper: therefore we freely give you, a few words of advice at this time.

We have heard it rumoured [rumored] abroad, that some at least, and probably many, are making their calculation to remove back to Kirtland next season.

Now brethren, this being the case, we advise you to abandon such an idea; yea we warn you, in the name of the Lord, not to remove back there, unless you are counseled so to do by the first Presidency, and the high council of Nauvoo. We do not wish by this to take your agency from you; but we feel to be plain, and pointed in our advice for we wish to do our duty, that your sins may not be found in our skirts. All persons are entitled to their agency for God has so ordained it.-He has constituted mankind moral agents, and given them power to chose good or evil; to seek after that which is good, by pursuing the pathway of holiness in this life, which brings peace of mind, and joy in the Holy Ghost here, and a fulness [fullness] of joy and happiness at his right hand hereafter; or to pursue an evil course, going on in sin and rebellion against God, thereby bringing condemnation to their souls in this world, and an eternal loss in the world to come. Since the God of heaven has left these things optional with every individual, we do not wish to deprive them of it. We only wish to act the part of a faithful watchman, agreeably to the word of the Lord to Ezekiel the prophet, Ezekiel 33 chap. 2 3 4 5 and verses, and leave it for others to do as seemeth them good.-Now for persons to do things, merely because they are advised to do them, and yet murmur all the time they are doing them, is of no use at all; they might as well not do them.

There are those who profess to be saints who are too apt to murmur, and find fault, when any advice is given, which comes in opposition to their feelings, even when they, themselves, ask for counsel; much more so when council is given unasked for, which does not agree with their notion of things; but brethren, we hope for better things from the most of you; we trust that you desire counsel, from time to time, and that you will cheerfully conform to it, whenever you r receive it from a proper source.

It is very probable, that it may be considered wisdom for some of us, and perhaps others, to move back to Kirtland, to attend to important business there: but notwithstanding that, after what we have written, should any be so unwise as to move back there, without being first counselled [counseled] so to do, their conduct will be highly disapprobated.

Done by order and vote of the first Presidency and high council for the Church of Jesus Christ of Latter Day Saints, at Nauvoo Dec. 8th 1839. H. G. SHERWOOD, Clerk.

Proceedings of the general Conference, held at Commerce, Hancock County, Illinois, on Saturday the 5th day of October, 1839.

The meeting was opened by prayer, by President Joseph Smith Jr. after which he was appointed president and James Sloan, Clerk of the Conference, by the unanimous voice of the meeting.

The President then spoke at some length upon the situation of the Church, the difficulties they had had to contend with, and the manner in which they had been led to this place; and wished to know the views of the brethren whether they wished to appoint this a stake or not, stating that he believed it to be a good place and suited for the saints.

It was then unauimously [unanimously] agreed upon, that it should be appointed a stake and a place of fathering for the saints. The following officers were then appointed viz:

William Marks to be President.--Bishop Whitney, to be bishop of Middle Ward.--Bishop Knight to be bishop of Lower Ward.

George W. Harris, Thomas Grover, Samuel Bent, Newel Knight,

Henry G. Sherwood, Charles C. Rich, David Fulmer, David Dort,

Alpheus Cutler, Seymour Brunson, Wm. Huntington, Lewis D. Wilson, to be high Council; who being respectfully called opon [upon], accepted af [of] their appointment.

It was then voted, that a branch of the Church be established on the other side of the river, in Iowa Territory; over which Elder John Smith was appointed President:

Alanson Ripley, Bishop, and

Asahel Smith, David Pettegrew, John M. Burke, Elijah Fordham,

A. Owen Smoot, Edward Fisher, Richard Howard, Elias Smith,

Willard Snow, John Patton, Erastus Snow, Stephen Chase,

Were elected high council.

Don C. Smith, was elected to be continued as President of the high Priesthood.

Orson Hyde to stand in his former office, and Willam Smith to be continued in his standing.

Letters were then read respecting the absence of Members, from ill health.

It was voted, that Harlow Redfield be suspended until he can have a trial, and in the meantime that he should not act as President of a branch, or preach.

Voted, that John Daley, James Daley and Milo Andrus retain their station in the church.

Voted that Ephraim Owens confession, for disobeying the word of wisdom be accepted.

Brothers,

Edward Johnston, William Allred, Benjamin Johnston, Wm. B. Simmons,

Samuel Musick, Wm. W. Edwards sr. John S. Fulmer, Wm. H. Edwards jr.

Jabez Lake, Hosea Stout, Benjamin Jones, Thomas Rich,

Henry OurBough, Allen J. Stout, Reddin Allred, Esiaias Edwards,

George W. Gee, John Adams, Jesse M'Intire, Daniel Miller,

James Brown, Simson I. Comfort, Henry Miller, Graham Coltrin,

Artemus Johnson, William Hyde, Joseph G. Hovey, Andrew Hendry,

Robert D. Foster, Redick N. Allred, Fields B. Jacamey, Eli Lee,

Zadock Bethers, Hiram W. Maxwell, and Thomas S. Edwards, were appointed Elders of the church, who all accepted of their appointment with the exception of Thomas S. Edwards.

John Gaylord, was admitted into the church upon his confession.

Abel Castro was confirmed by the laying on of hands.

The meeting then adjourned until Sunday Morning after which six were baptized by Joseph Smith Jr.

Sunday October the 6th.-----The Conference met pursuant to adjournment at 8 o'clock, A. M..

When,

Samuel Williams, Reuben Foot, Orlando D. Hovey, Junis Rappleyee,

Sheffield Daniels, Albert Miner, David B. Smith, Ebe'r Richardson,

Pleasant Ewell, William Helm,

Were appointed Elders of the church and were ordained under the hands of Reynolds Cahoon, Seymour Brunson, Samuel Bent and Alpheus Cutler.

After some remarks from the President respecting observing order andecorum [indecorum] during conference, Elder Lyman Wight, spoke as to the dutiesod [of] Priests, Teachers, tc [etc.].

President J. Smith, Jr. then spoke as to appointing a Patriarch and other matters connected with the well being of the church. Having now got through the business matters, the President proceeded to give instructions to the Elders respecting preaching the gospel, and pressed upon them the necessity of getting the Spirit, so that they might preach with the Holy Ghost sent down from heaven, to be careful in speaking on those subjects which are not clearly pointed out in the word of God, which lead to speculation and strife.

Those person who had been baptized were then confirmed, and several children received blessings by Elders Bent, Cutler and Brunson. Elder Lyman Wight then addressed the meeting, on the subject of raising funds by contribution, towards paying for the lands which had been contracted for, as a settlement for the church, after which contributions were received for that purpose.

Judge Higbee, was appointed to accompany Presidents J. Smith, Jr. and S. Rigdon, to the City of Washington.

The meeting then adjourned until Monday morning.

Monday morning October the 9th.

Conference met pursuant to adjournment.

The President spoke at some length to the Elders, and explained many passages of scripture.

Elder Lyman Wight spoke on the subject of the resurection [resurrection], and other important subjects. When he offered the following resolution, which passed unanimously:

Resolved, That a new edition of Hymn Books be printed immediately, and that the one published by D. W. Rogers, be utterly discarded by the church.

Elder Ezra Hayes was then put upon trial for teaching doctrine injurious to the church, and for falsehoods; which having been proved against him his license was withdrawn and he required to give satisfaction to those whom he had offended.

Charges having been prefered [preferred] against Brother Rogers, it was agreed that the case be handed over to the high council.

Asahel Perry made application to be received into fellowship, and was voted into his former standing.

After having referred the business not gone into, to the high council; the president then returned thanks to the conference for their good attention and liberality; and having blessed them in the name of the Lord, the conference was dismissed.

The next conference was appointed to be held on the 6th day of April next.

A Conference was held at the house of Brother Benjamin Wilcox in McDonough county, Ill. on the 2nd day of June, 1839 for the purpose of organizing a church. Meeting was opened by Elder Coltrin, after which Elder D. C. Smith rose and after making known the object of the meeting nominated Elder Coltrin, President who was unanimously chosen, and John Vance, was appointed secretary. And after adjusting some small matters of difficulties, proceeded to appoint Arctes Geer, Priest , Heny Hoyt Teacher, and John Sagers, Deacon, when some three or four children were brought forward and blessed in the church, and after dismission one was baptized. This church consists of sixty nine members in good standing. Z. COLTRIN, Pres't. JOHN VANCE, Clerk.

September 1st, 2839

    Met in conferance [conference], at the house of Brother Isaac Chace, in Sparta, for the purpose of organizing a branch of the church of Christ of Latter Day Saints in that place. Elder H. Kellogg was called to the chair, and J. F. Olney chosen Clerk. When Elder Ezra Chace was appointed to preside over the same and Brother Isaac Chace was ordained to the office of Deacon; and 25 persons were enrolled as members.

    MARRIED-In this place, on the 24th of Sept. by Elder Don C. Smith. William D. Huntington, to Miss Caroline Clark.

    Also, in this place, on the 7th of Oct. by Elder Don C. Smith, James Moses, to Miss Eliza Spencer, both of Rushville, Ill.

For the Times and Seasons.

THE SLAUGHTER ON SHOAL CREEK,

CALDWELL COUNTY MISSOURI.

[BY MISS ELIZA R. SNOW.]

    Here, in a land that freemen call their home, And at the shadowy close of parting day,

    Far from the influence of papal Rome; In slaughter'd heaps, husbands and fathers lay;

    Yes, in a "mild and tolerating age" There lay the dead and there the dying ones

    The saint have fall'n beneath the barb'rous rage The air reverberating with their groans;

    Of men inspired, by that misjudging hate, Night's sable sadness mingling with the sound

Which ignorance and prejudice create; Spread a terriffic hideousness around;

Ill-fated men-whose minds would hardly grace Ye wives and mothers; think of women then

The most ferocious of the brutal race:- Left in a group of dead, and dying men,

Men without hearts-else, would their bosoms bleed Her hopes were blasted-all her prospects riv'n

At the commission of so foul a deed Save one; she trusted in the God of heav'n,

As that, when they, at Shoal Creek, in Caldwell, Long, for the dead, her widow'd heart will crave

Upon an unresisting people fell; A last kind office-yes, A DECENT GRAVE!

Whose only crime, was, DARING TO PROFESS Description fails; Tho' language is too mean

THE ETERNAL PRINCIPLES OF RIGHTEOUSNESS To paint the horrors of that dreadful scene,

Twas not enough for that unfeeling crew, All things are present to His searching eye

To murder men: they shot them through and through? Whose ears are open to the ravens' cry.

Frantic with rage; they pour'd their moulted lead.

For mercies claim, which heav'n delights to hear

Profusely on the dying and the dead;

Fell disregarded on relentless ears;

Long o'er the scene, of that unhappy eve

Will the lone widow-and the orphan grieve

Their savage foes, with greedy av'rice fir'd;

Plunder'd their murder'd victims, and retir'd;

OBITUARY.-DIED-In this place on the 8th of July Zina, consort of William Huntington, aged 53 years.

-In this place, Sept. 22nd, Orin Rockwell, aged 55 years.

-In this place, Nov. 2nd, Mahew Hillman, aged 46 years.

-In this place on the 26th, of July, Sterry Fisk aged 41 years.

-In this place, Oct. 7th, Hezekiah W. Fisk, aged 30 Years

-In Pittsfield, Pike co. Ill. September 13th, Silas Smith, aged 58 years.

-Near Carthage, in this county, about the 8th of September last, Jesse Robinson, aged 40 years.

-In this place, Oct. 3d, Nancy Rigdon, aged 80 years.

-In this place, Nov. 24th, Mr.Akins from Peoria, Ill.

-In this place, Nov. 6th, Rhoda, consort of Hezekiah Fisk, aged 62 years.

-In this place, Nov. 9th, Hezekiah Fisk, aged 64 years;

-In this place, Nov. 11th, William Fisk aged 35 years.

-In this place, Nov. 3d, James Mulholland, aged 35 years.

-In this place, Nov. 13th, Lucy Ives, (a widow) aged 57 years.

-In this place, July 14th. Harriet Maria, Daughter of Sterry and Maria P. Fisk aged 8 months and 8 days.

-In this place, Nov. 26th. Dinah, daughter of Stephen and Hanna Markham, aged 12 years 8 months, and 26 days.

-In this place, Oct. 19th, Hiram, Infant son of Hiram and Thankful Clark, aged 7 weeks.-

-At Clayton on the 22nd of June last, Charity, consort of Ira Ames, aged 32 years.

-At Pittsfield Pike co. July 23rd, Rebeckah, consort of M. B. Welton.

-At Sackets Harbor. N. Y. Oct. 16th, Mary Norris, aged 19 years.

-In this place, Nov. 24th, Mr. Akins from Peoria Ill.

-At Henderson, Jefferson co. N. Y. Oct. 3d, Cyrus Bates, in the 28th year of his age.

-At Sparta, Livingston co. N. Y. on the 28th of Aug. Elizabeth, consort of Elder Charles Thompson.

-At Montrose, Lee co. Iowa, Infant child Lydia, daughter of Orson and Sally M. Pratt, aged 8 months 8 days.

-At Quincy, Ill. on the 10th day of May last, Maryett, daughter of Dimick B. and Fanny Huntington, aged 3 years.

-In this place, Sept. 15th, Martha, daughter of John D. and Harriet Parker, aged 10 months and 10 days.

THE TIMES AND SEASONS Is printed and published every month, at Commerce, Hancock co. Ill. by E. ROBINSON AND D. C. SMITH, Editors and Proprietors.

TERMS, One dollar per annum, payable, in all cases, in advance. Any person procuring 10 subscribers, and forwarding us ten dollars current money, shall receive one volume gratis. All current Bank notes, of any denomination will be received on subscriptions. Letters on business must be addressed to the Publishers, POST PAID.

TIMES AND SEASONS

"TRUTH WILL PREVAIL"

Vol. 1. Whole No. 3.] COMMERCE, ILLINOIS, JANUARY, 1840 [Whole No. 3.

A HISTORY, OF THE PERSECUTION, OF THE CHURCH OF JESUS CHRIST, OF LATTER DAY SAINTS IN MISSOURI.

CONTINUED.

Saturday, Nov. 2d, it was concluded to try again for a peace warrant: accordingly application was made to a magistrate by the name of Silvers, who resided some distance from town, and who had not as yet openly joined the mob, but he refused to grant a warrant, saying that if he did he feared that his life would be in danger.-The next day four men were started to the circuit judge, forty miles distance, after considerable delay by the judge, they obtained warrants against a number of individuals. When the warrants arrived, it was too late to do any thing with them, for the whole county was getting up in arms, and the saints had as much as they could do to take care of themselves. But to return-Saturday night came on, and a party of the mob went to a settlement of the saints living on Big Blue river about six miles west of town; they first tore the roof from a house, and injured the furniture within; they then divided their company into two parties, one went to pulling the roof from another dwelling house, whilst the other party went to another and broke it open; they found the owner D. Bennett in bed, whom they took and beat unmercifully; one of the company drew a pistol, and swore that he would blow out his brains, but the ball laid bare his skull without fracturing it-thus narrowly he escaped with his life. A party of the saints were collected near by, who hearing the disturbance went to the place. The mob began to fire upon them, and they returned the compliment, a few guns were discharged from both parties, but the fire was not general; at length a young man of the mob was shot in the thigh, and soon after the mob dispersed for that night.

Sunday, Nov. 3d. Many threatnings were heard from the mobbers; they were greatly enraged, and were exerting themselves to strengthen their party; for as yet some of the inhabitants manifested friendship for the brethren; such told them, that they expected, they would all be massacre, for the enemy were about to get a six pounder and come out openly against them the next day.

Monday, Nov. 4th. A large mob collected at Wilson's store. about a mile west of Big Blue, they came to the Blue took the ferry boat, and threatened some lives; but for some unknown cause, perhaps to take some more whiskey, they left the Blue and returned to Wilson's store again.-Whilst they were at the Blue threatening the saints, word was sent to a body of the brethren, about five or six miles distant to the southwest, that a large mob was collected, and they expected that they should need help; whereupon nineteen brethren started to go and assist them, but before they reached Wilson's store, they learned that the mob had returned there, upon hearing this, they proceeded no farther, but returned back. The mob, by some means feared that they were on the road west of them; when from fifty to seventy of the mob took their rifles, mounted their horses, and went in pursuit of them: after traveling about two miles they came in sight of them, when they all fled into the cornfields and woods; some went immediately to the body, and informed their brethren, of what they had seen. About thirty of the saints, (mostly those who had lived in the settlement, where the mob then was, some of whom had had their housed unroofed, but a short time before,) took their arms, and started as soon as possible to meet the mob.-Meantime the mob turned their horses into cornfields, of the saints, and then hunted for them who had fled; they went to C. Whitmers a lame brother, who had not left his home, and pointed their guns at him, and threatened his life, provided he did not tell them where his brethren had fled to. They also threatened women and children. In this manner they spent their time for about an hour, when about sundown a company, of thirty brethren, marched up, and as soon as they came near enough, the mob fired upon them, and they immediately fired back; after a round or two, the mob retreated and left the ground; they were followed a short distance, but not far.

Two of the mob, and a number of horses were killed, and some five or six wounded. The mob were so frightened, that they left their dead on the ground over night. The saints had four or five wounded, one by the name of Barber mortally, who died the next day. P. Dibble was wounded, in the bowels by the first gun fired.

The same day at Independence, A. S. Gilbert, I Morley, J. Corrill, and Wm. E. McLelin were taken for assault and battery, and false imprisonment by McCarty, whom they had taken the Friday night previous. And although they could not get a warrant for him, for breaking the store, yet he had obtained one for them, for catching him at it.

They were prisoners in the court house, on trial, when news of the battle reached town. It was stated, that the Mormons had killed twenty of the mob, and had gone to Wilson's and shot his son. In a moment as it were, all was confusion in the house. The majority were for massacreing [massacring] the prisoners forthwith; but a few, more human then the rest, were not willing to see prisoners murdered, while in open court, they advised them to go to jail to save their lives; this they did, and were hurried, but with difficulty protected by those few friends, to the jail; where they felt happy to be locked in. They were visited by some influential men, who told them that the mob had now become desperate, and that the whole county had become enraged, and nothing would stop them from massacreing [massacring] the whole society but to leave the county forthwith. About midnight the sheriff, with two other men, went with Morley, Corrill and Gilbert to visit their brethren who were collected near town. A short consultation was held with some of them, when it was agreed that they should leave the county immediately and use their influence with their brethren, to have them go also. These were times which tried men's souls; to stay where they were was death, and to undertake to remove so large a body at once, there being about ten or twelve hundred of them, looked like destruction of much property, if not of lives. It seemed, however to be the only alternative; and property at that time was no object. If they could but obtain sufficient to live upon, they chose rather to wander off into some lonely wilderness, or even descent where they could enjoy peace, than to stay where they were, even if they could, and be continually harrassed [harassed] as they had been for a few months past. But to return to the thread of our story, the party in returning back to jail, were met at the jail, by a company of mobbers who were disposed to kill the prisoners in spite of the sheriff and his assistants; Morley and Corrill seeing their danger, broke and run, but were fired at; Gilbert had two guns snapped at him, one of which flashed in the pan; he was then knocked down, but not injured so but that with the help of the sheriff and his assistants he soon got into the jail, where he felt himself measurably safe. Early next morning the prisoners were discharged. It was afterwards acknowledged by the enemy that they had intended to have taken the leading men for some pretended crime. a few at a time until they got them all, ahd [had] shut them up in prison; and then to have fallen upon the rest and drove them out of the county and then sent the leaders after them.

The saints were such abominable characters, doing so many wicked things which the law could not reach, that they had become very obnoxious, to the good people of Jackson county, who were so pious, so moral and so loyal to the constitution and laws of our country, that they would not live with them, but must thrust them out: Whereas, if any, even the most abandoned amongst the saints would leave the Church, deny the faith take a good dram of whiskey, swear and blaspheme the name of God roundly, they could be permitted to stay, they were hail fellows well met. They made the offer themselves, that if any would deny the faith and leave the church, they might stay and be protected there; and a number tried the experiment with success; and it is believed that some few of them are living there in peace, to this day.

We will return again to the night of the battle. The mob sent their runners over the county, to stir up the feelings of the people, by misrepresenting the doings of the saints, so as to have them all turn out, and exterminate them at once. The people took their arms and started for Independence, as fast as they possibly could, so that early the next morning there were hundreds there ready for war. Col. Pitcher pretended to call out the militia, as he said to quell the mob, and make peace between the parties; but the fact is he put himself, or was put, some said by L. W. Boggs, then lieutenant Gov., at the head of the mob, for the purpose of making a show of legality for what they did.

We must now return again to the evening after the battle, and bring up another item. The body of saints near Independence, learning in the evening, that the brethren were shut up in the jail, and as they supposed for the purpose of being put to death, sent word immediately to Br. L. Wight, (who lived about six miles off,) of their situation, and requested help. Colonel Wight collected together a hundred or more of the saints, who were but poorly armed, some having no weapons, but clubs, and in the morning marched them on the road towards Independence expecting to stop at the camp of the saints, near town; but hearing of the release of the prisoners, and of the agreement of the brethren to leave the county forthwith; and also that the militia were called out at Independence to make peace, before he had reached the brethren's settlement, he turned aside his men into the woods, concluding to disperse soon and go home. News flew to town, that Wight with a company of his brethren, were marching towards that place; this so enraged Col. Pitcher, and his pretended militia, that he demanded that Wight and his company should give up their arms; and also those men who were in the battle the night before, should be given up, to be tried for murder; saying that if they would do those things, they should be safely protected, whilst removing out of the county; otherwise there was no peace for them. They reluctantly consented to these propositions, and were it not for fear of resisting the authorities of the country, they would sooner have shed their blood in the defence [defense] of their rights, and the liberty of their country, than to have submitted to such oppression. However the arms were given up, amounting to fifty one guns, one sword and one pistol. And a number of those who were in the battle, gave themselves up as prisoners. The Saints then made all possible exertions to leave the county. After detaining the prisoners a day and a night, and pretending to try them for murder; and also threatening and brick batting them, Col. Pitcher took them into a cornfield, so that their lives would not be in danger, from his pretended militia; and after taking a watch from one of them for costs, he being the constable, said to them "clear." Col. Pitcher promised to give back the brethren's arms, whenever they left the county, this he afterwards refused to do; Whereupon the Governor's order was twice obtained for them but he would not obey it, neither have they ever been paid for. The saints concluded to move south, into Van Buren county, which was consented to by a number of the leading men. But before night word was sent to them that they might go north and east, but south and west they must not go, if they did, they would meet with trouble.

Wednesday, Nov. 6, the arms having been taken from the saints; the mob now felt safe, and were no longer militia, they formed themselves into companies, and went forth on horse-back armed, to harrass [harass] the saints, and take all the arms they could find. Two of these companies were headed by baptist preachers. The Rev. Isaac McCoy, headed one about seventy, the other priest' company, whose name is not now recollected, contained from thirty to forty. They went forth through the different settlements of the saints, threatening them with death, and distruction [destruction] if they were not off immediately. They broke open houses, and plundered them, where they found them shut, and the owners gone. As it happened the men were mostly gone from home that day; making arrangements for getting away. The mob that day stripped some of the saints of their arms, even to penknives; some they whipped; they shot at some and others they hunted after; as they said to kill them.

Mobs. well lined with whiskey, as these were, looking and acting worse than savages, were well calculated to frighten women and children; which they effectually did in some cases.-One settlement were so frightened, that a party of from 130 to 150, women and children, with only six men to protect them, not waiting the return of their husbands and fathers, left their homes forthwith on foot, without taking any of their things, and wandered off south, upon the prairie a number of days under the broad canopy of heaven, not knowing which way the church was intending to go. The stubs of the newly burnt grass, and weeds, were so hard that they cut the feet of the children, who had no shoes, so that many of them became very sore, and bled profusely. Other companies fled towards the Missouri river; and in a short time the most of the church, were under way for Clay county; some few went east, and others south. After some of the head men had left, and the saints were generally getting under way, the mob in a measure ceased to harrass [harass] them. The people of Clay county received the saints, with as much hospitality as could be expected. The loses and sacrifices of the saints, were very great in the destruction of crops, furniture, clothing, &c. and also in the loss of stock. Grain and many other things, would hardly bear transportation across the river; consequently much was left behind, that otherwise might have been got away.

After it was thought that the mob spirit had died away, some few families moved back from Van Buren county to their former homes in Jackson; where what they had for the sustainance [sustenance] of themselves, and their stock was.

They had not long been back, before a mob party visited them in the night; and took some of the men and beat them with chairs and clubs till life was nearly extinct, and then left them for dead; one by the name of Leonard, was a long time recovering; indeed he has never fully recovered from that beating.

There were four aged families in Jackson, who had not left their homes, whose age, infirmities and penury seemed to say, you may tarry until the spring opens; but neither age nor infirmities, would protect a saint in Jackson county. These veterans, the youngest of the four being 94 years of age, were assailed by a mob party, who broke in their doors and windows, hurling large stones into their houses, whereby, some of their lives were greatly endangered; and thus they were driven from their homes, in the winter season. Some of these men have toiled and bled, in the defence [defense] of their country; one of them (Mr. Jones,) served as life guard to General Washington in the revolutionary war.

COMMUNICATIONS.

Messrs, Editors, of the Times and Seasons, For the benefit of the church, and the public in general, please give the following an insertion in your valuable periodical.

In consequence of being deeply involved with others of my brethren, in establishing and locating a place for the saints, I have not availed myself of the opportunity of laying before the public, the principal cause of the calamities which bursted upon the saints in Far West. I shall not attempt at this time to give a history of the sufferings of the saints for it would require a volume. But as the inquiry is often made, and the cause of the imprisonment of the leaders of the church frequently called for; it becomes my duty as a member of the church, to state to the public, that not only traitorism, but treachery, cowardice, and perjury, G. M. Hinkle and other apostates together with a predetermined resolution of the mob, and land pirates of the upper Missouri, are the leading items, and most prominent features of all the calamities which bursted upon the saints in Far West, and also the cause of the imprisonment of the leaders of the church.

In the first place, I will endeavor to exhibit to the understanding of the public the conduct of G. M. Hinkle a commander of the militia, in Caldwell county, and known as a preacher in the church for years: he commanded the militia in Caldwell co. until he betrayed the leaders of the church into the hands of the mob. Mr. Corrill calls them militia, but if the stealing of cattle, horses, hogs; burning waggons [wagons], and carrying off all kinds of property; warrants them that appellation I have no objection, I appeal to the public to name them.

And after G. M. Hinkle and others had agreed to deliver up the leaders, and give up arms &c. they declared that they (the leaders of the church) must be immediately shot, for they delivered them up on no other conditions; fearing that their traitorism and cowardice might be more fully exposed.

The mob then forced them immediately into their camp, and the treatment that they received there, would make the blood thirsty savage of the wilderness blush, or the wandering Arab hide his face for shame. They then held what they termed a court martial over them, and they were condemned to be shot; but fortune favors the innocent, the God of Israel was there and protected them; so that they did not carry their murderous purposes into execution, for they began to see that it was cold blooded murder, and that Uncle Sam would inquire into the affair.

There were seventeen officers who composed this court martial, and twelve out of seventeen consented to the death of these men, but thank God there was virtue enough in the minority, to overrule the infamy of the majority, therefore their lives were spared.

They then manufactured a plan to cast them into prison, they therefore appealed to civil authority as they termed it; but if the court over which Austin A. King presided was civil authority, may the Lord deliver me from uncivil authority, for if a man did not testify as he or Birch, the states Attorney taught him, he was thrust into prison and totally deprived of his testimony.

However, they were taken before Austin king, a Judge of the fifth Judicial circuit of the State of Missouri for trial, and the testimony of Hinkle and other apostates was called for, and if the testimony of these men could be exhibited to the public as it was recorded by the court, they would then be convinced that it would puzzle any thing else but a Missouri lawyer to arrange such nonsense as was sworn to by Hinkle and others, so as to make it a sufficient tool to commit free citizens of the United States to jail, for the testimony from beginning to end was known to be as black as the ace of spades, and as false as the tales of Valentine and Orson. A. RIPLEY.

Extract from a letter written by E. Partridge, to his brother Samuel, but for certain reasons was never sent.

Quincy, Adams co. Ill. May 26, 1839. Since I saw you I have passed through some trying scenes; but all the persecution that is heaped upon us, only goes to prove that we are not of the world. The Saviour [Savior] said to his disciples, "If ye were of the world, the world would love his own." When I look at the 11th. chap. of Hebrews, and there see what the ancient saints had to endure, that they might obtain a better resurrection; and when I read in the Revelations of John, 7th chap. of a great company arrayed in white robes whom he saw before the throne of God, serving him day and night, who had come up through great tribulation; I say in my heart, how many in this age of the world, will be among the number? Who, among all the professors of religion throughout Christendom except Latter Day Saints, can say that they have had to pass through great tribulation? Let them compare their sufferings with the ancients, who were tortured, were stoned, were sawn asunder, were tempted, were slain with the sword; who wandered about in sheep skins and goat skins; being destitute, afflicted and tormented; (of whom the world was not worthy:) Who wandered in deserts, and mountains, and dens, and caves of the earth, and not more than one in a hundred can (in righteousness) say that they have. well if this is a fact, and, who will attempt to deny it? is not the religious world deceived or deceiving themselves? Surely they will not form a part of that company who came up through great tribulation.

Perhaps you may think that I am mistaken, and that in consequence of milder government, persecution has measurably ceased; and that now it is not necessary to pass through great tribulation, to be a part of that number. Paul's words are, All that will live Godly in Christ Jesus shall suffer persecution. And I am confident that the same cause will produce the same effect; and that the pure religion of Jesus Christ will be followed by persecution. Let us examine Paul's words closely, All that will live Godly *in Christ Jesus*, not out of Christ Jesus, shall suffer persecution. Paul does not say all or any, who live Godly out of Christ Jesus shall suffer persecution. And I consider that there is a great difference between in and out.

Perhaps you may ask is there any who live Godly, out of Christ Jesus? I answer yes, measurably so at least; there are honorable men who never make a profession of religion, or are baptized, who are exemplary men, who love the principles of truth and righteousness, justice and mercy, and who are truly ornaments to society.-They are Godlike, or in other words live Godly lives, but never put on Christ, because their minds are blinded by the craftiness of men. Perhaps you may ask who are in Christ Jesus? I will let Paul answer the question. In writing to his Galatian brethren, 3d chap. he says, "Ye are all the children of God by faith in Christ Jesus.-For as many of you as have been baptized *into Christ* have *put on Christ.* There is neither Jew nor Greek, there is neither bond nor free, there is neither male nor female; for ye are all one in Christ Jesus. And if ye be Christ's then ye are *Abraham's seed* and *heirs according to the promise.*" Perhaps you may say that the most of the religious world have been baptized into Christ. If so, I ask by whom, and by what authority? If you answer by the ministers or priests of the different persuasions, and that they have their authority from God.

I then ask when and where did they get their authority from God? Not direct of course, for they deny that any have received revelations since the days of the apostles, and there is none that can trace their authority back to the apostles, without going through the church of Rome, therefore their authority is no better than the Pope's.-It appears to me to be a fact, clear as the sun at noon day, that it became absolutely necessary that God should again reveal himself to man and confer authority upon some one, or more, before his church could be built up in the last days, or at any time after the apostacy [apostasy].

The authority of the priesthood is a subject that I did not look into, until sometime after I was convinced that there was not a true church, according to the Bible, among all the churches of my acquaintance. And when I discovered that they were all without authority from God, I was doubly confirmed in my opinion.

The church of Jesus Christ of Latter day Saints believes that God has revealed himself, through Jesus Christ to man again, and conferred the Priesthood or authority, upon his servants in this age, as in ancient days. And for this faith we are persecuted; and this we expect. Yet, still we are determined to live Godly in Christ Jesus, persecution or no persecution, tribulation or no tribulation, because we greatly desire to inherit a celestial glory: Yea we count all earthly pleasures but dross, when compared with that glory which is to be revealed, which eye has not seen, nor ear heard, neither entered into the heart of man to conceive of, which is laid up for those who love and serve God with full purpose of heart. Celestial glory is what we are seeking after, and to obtain it we are willing to suffer some afflictions, for we believe that it cannot be obtained by us upon any other principle. But if you, or any other person can attain to a celestial glory without being persecuted, or passing through great tribulation; I have no objection: but I fear that those who take the smooth road, will find in the end of this life, that it leads to another place. It appears to me to be a law of heaven, that the seed of Abraham should have their faith tried, similar to what his was; because I believe, that God is a reasonable being, and would not require more of Abraham, according to his abilities, than he would require of others, who were to inherit the same glory. The Lord has said of his children in our day, "They must needs be chastened, and tried, even as Abraham, who was commanded to offer up his only son; for all those who will not endure chastening, but deny me, cannot be sanctified." And this agrees with the Bible, Heb. 2nd chap. 10th verse. "For it became him for whom are all things, and by whom are all things, in bringing many sons unto glory, to make the captain of their salvation perfect through sufferings.-"For both he that sanctifieth and they who are sanctified are all one." Also the 5th chap. 8 and 9th verses, "Though he were a son, yet he learned obedience by the things which he suffered; and being made perfect, he became the author of eternal salvation unto all them that obey him." Also, from the 19th chap., "My son despise not thou the chastening of the Lord, nor faint when thou art rebuked of him. For whom the Lord loveth he chasteneth, God dealeth with you as with sons; for what son is he whom the father chasteneth not? But if ye be without chastisement whereof all are partakers, then are ye bastards and not sons."-Admitting that the apostle has told us the truth in the above extract, I ask what portion of the religious world, at the present day are entitled to the appellation of sons? And also what proportion must come under the head of bastards? I would also ask, do bastards become heirs; or are they not generally despised and cast off? These questions I leave you to answer for yourself.

But for one I am free to say, I am convinced that a great majority of the professors of religion are not sons of God, nor heirs of a celestial glory, but are bastards & as such will receive their reward whether it be good or evil. I do not say this because, I wish to hurt any person's feelings, but rather that I might stimulate my fellow travelers to eternity, to examine the subject more fully than they have heretofore. I feel sorry for them, and pity them, because I believe many of them are honest, and verily think that they are sons and heirs of God, but are blinded by the cunning craftiness of men., and the traditions of their fathers.

Oh! that those chains of tradition and superstition, that bind so many of the human family, might be broken, and their minds set at liberty; that they may expand as broad as eternity, and as high as the throne of God, that they may increase in wisdom and knowledge, until they can comprehend the vast creations of God: even until they can see as they are seen, and know as they known.

Detroit City, Sept. 18, 1839. TO THE PUBLISHERS OF THE TIMES AND SEASONS.

I hereby transmit to you a short account of my labours [labors] in the State of Michigan this season; myself in conjunction with other elders have preached much in parts of Wayne, Washtenaw, Lenawee, Oakland and Lapeer counties, I have been present and assisied [assisted] in ordaining proper officers, and organizing thereby the following branches; viz: one at Macon, Lenawee County two in Wayne County, in the towns of Livonia and Van Buren and one in Lapeer, Lapeer county, the branches now contain about 60 members among whom we have ordained 5 elders, 4 priests, I have laboured [labored] for the most part with Elder A. Blanchard and may God bless our testimony unto those who have heard and not as yet obeyed, may it be found to have produced fruit after many days. Man being by nature always the same, and we having examples of what hath been done in times past, may calculate on the present, and future; therefore while a few have believed the gospel, loved God and obeyed him, many have believed, loved the world and neglected so great a salvation, and perhaps may stand still, for fear the work of God will come to naught, till the angel of death shall seal them his.

And many have disbelieved the gospel altogether; some few in Plymouth Wayne county, go so far as to disturb public worship, with drums, fifes, horns, bells, ridiculous gestures and horrid yells, and some of them too, professing Godliness, and others whose parents profess to bring up their soes [sons] in the nurture and admonition of the Lord, and have them initiated in their infancy. In Lapeer village, some went so far as to fill a house in time of worship with tobacco smoke and also, that of powder by firing fire crackers in the house, also saluting the house outwardly with a gun; there were two magistrates and one constable present, officers, sworn to keep the peace who looked quietly on, and said nothing to the rabble, and I learn that at least one if not both of the magistrates assisted in disturbing the public and the harmony of the worship of God; "the Lord reward them according to their works." The following Sabbath I had the privilege of leading three into the waters of baptism, may the Lord bless them and preserve them for his kingdom.

I am now on my way home having been absent between four and five months. STEPHEN POST.

A copy of a letter dated, Iowa Territory, Jan. 4, 1840.

Sir.-You informed me that a committee of Mormons are about to apply to Congress of the United States, for an investigation on the cause of their expulsion from the State of Missouri, and to ask of the general Government remuneration for the losses sustained by them in consequence of such expulsion, and ask of me to state my opinion of the character and general conduct of these people while they resided in the State of Ohio: and also the conduct and general report of those who have settled in the Territory of Iowa, since their expulsion from The State of Mo.

In compliance with your request, I will state that I have had but little personal acquaintance with them: I know that there was a community of them in the north part of the State of Ohio, and while I resided in the State, they were generally considered an industrious, inoffensive people; and I have no recollection of ever having heard, in that State of their being charged with violating the laws of the country.

Since their expulsion from Missouri a portion of them, about one hundred families, have settled in Lee county, Iowa Territory, and are generally considered industrious, inoffensive and worthy citizens.

Very respectfully yours,

ROBERT LUCAS;

A. RIPLY GOV. OF IOWA TER.

TIMES AND SEASONS COMMERCE, ILL. JAN. 1840

NEW YEARS ADDRESS. We have arrived at the close of another year. Yes, 1839 has passed away and gone. And since its commencement, thousands of our fellow mortals have gone to try the realities of another world, yet we are spared: and we have abundant reason to thank the God who made us, and who has upheld us to the present time, for the mercies and blessings which he has bestowed upon us, unworthy creatures as we are.

In taking a retrospective view of the past, we see many things, respecting ourselves, which we could wish had been otherwise; but still for the most part, we have kept a conscience void of offence [offense] towards God and man.

Our brethren, the saints, have had to pass through much affliction, and sorrow the past year: thousands of them have had to leave a goodly land, a healthy land, and a pleasant land; yea a land which they had bought, and had paid for; and had also made for themselves comfortable homes, upon the same; that we say they had to leave. Yes and in the cold and dreary months of winter too; being subjected to many privations, whilst journeying hundreds of miles, in that inclement season of the year. And we have no doubt, but that many have been brought to an untimely grave, and that hundreds of others have experienced more or less sickness, in consequence of the privations, troubles and hardships which they have had to endure. Which privations were brought upon them by the barbarous conduct of a jealous, unfeeling, and hard-hearted people: whom the saints never injured, neither had they any desire so to do, provided they could have been left, to enjoy their own fireside in peace. But notwithstanding the great persecution of the saints, still the work rolls on, and many are embracing it for the truth's sake; which shows that the cause of God will prevail, in spite of men or devils.

But the year is past and gone, and the earth continues to roll on its axis as usual; and the great mass of mankind pass down the stream of time, as thoughtless and as giddy, as though they were certain that there was no God no eternity, no heaven or hell, and no happiness or misery beyond this life. They have no time for reflection; snd [and] they are so engaged in business, their minds so engrossed with the cares of this life, the obtaining of riches and honors, that they do not realize, that time is passing swiftly away, and soon will hurry them off the stage of action, to make room for others, perhaps as thoughtless and careless as they. There are many, no doubt, even among this class, who partially believe in God, and divine things, who have such an imperfect idea, of the character of the great Jehovah; and such an undue attachment, to the perishable things of time and sense, that they think it a hardship to serve him while in youth or middle age, but who think that they will attend to that, when old age arrives, and the world has no more allurements for them. Yet did they but realize, that God was the most lovely, of all things which exist, whether animate or inanimate, they would see the propriety of that command which says, "Thou shalt love the Lord, thy God with all thy soul, might, mind and strength." They would not put off the service of God, but would with the Psalmist say. Now is the accepted time, and, now is the day of salvation. And as one of old said, would say.-As for me, and my house, we will serve the Lord.

In looking back, over the past year, we see that the world of mankind appear to grow worse and worse, wickeder and wickeder. They seem to be determined, more than ever before, to build themselves up in wealth, and fame, upon the ruin of each other.- Steam boats and rail-road cars are caused to strive, to outvie others in speed, that they may obtain advantage over them, whilst thousands of lives are endangered theyeby [thereby], and accident upon accident are happening in consequence thereof. Flatteries and deceptions, of almost every kind, are practised [practiced]; by many at the present day, to gain a favorite object. The mind and ingenuity of man is constantly on the stretch, to invent ways legally to injure, overreach, and defraud, the honest and unsuspecting: and when it cannot be done legally, there are not wanting men, who will resort to illegal means, to accomplish their end.

We see that men, still continue to get intoxicated, notwithstanding all the exertions made to reform them: and lying is so common, that at present, it is hardly considered a vice. The depravity of the human heart may be seen in looking over the columns of the newspapers of the day; for we there discover that all manner of crimes are practised [practiced] to a very great extent. It seems as though they had increased beyond a parallel, for a few years past. Swindling, pilfering, counterfeiting, robbing; burglary, arson, and murder are committed with the greatest boldness and have increased to an alarming degree, within a few years, especially in the cities. No man who travels alone feels safe at the present day, who has much money about his person. How often travelers are robbed of pocket books, trunks, &c. And many a man has been murdered, even within the past year, for his money; and in some cases for paltry sums. The merchant finds it very difficult to so guard his store, that his goods will not frequently be taken by some arch fiend in human form; and no property of value is safe except strongly secured by bars and bolts. Formerly in this country, these things were not so; the great body of the people were honest, and iniquity had to hide its head. And now according to the present ratio in morals, we would ask, how long will it take the sectarian world to bring about the *Millenium*, upon the principles which they go upon, of converting and making saints, or christians of all the inhabitants of the earth? contrary to the plain declarations of scripture. And here let us quote three of four testimonies to prove our assertion. And first, "Behold the day of the Lord cometh, cruel both with wrath and fierce anger to lay the land desolate; and he shall destroy the sinners thereof out of it." Isaiah XIII. 9. Again, "The earth also is defiled under the inhabitants thereof; because they have transgressed the laws, changed the ordinance, broken the everlasting covenant. Therefore hath the curse devoured the earth, and they that dwell therein are desolate: therefore the inhabitants of the earth are burned, and few men left." Isaiah XXIV, 5 and 6, and again, "And to you who are troubled, rest with us, when the Lord Jesus shall be revealed from heaven with his mighty angels, in flaming fire taking vengeance on them that know not God, and obey not the gospel of our Lord Jesus Christ." 2nd Thess. 1; 7 and 8, and also Paslms XXXVII, 8, 9 10 and 11 verses, "cease from anger, and forsake wrath: fret not thyself in any wise to do evil.- For evil doers shall be cut off; but those that wait upon the Lord, they shall inherit the earth. For yet a little while and the wicked shall not be: yea, thou shalt dilligently [diligently] consider his place, and it shall not be. But the meek shall inherit the earth; and shall delight themselves in the abundance of peace." Let these passages of scripture suffice for the present on the subject of the Millenium.

Eighteen hundred forty has arrived, and we wish mankind generally, but more particularly our friends, patrons, a year of happiness; but of this we have no assurances to offer them. We will not pretend to predict, what lies in the bosom of futurity, to be unfolded the present year, further than that we have no doubt, but what there will be many births, many marriages, and many deaths. Many, no doubt will be called to lay down this tenement of clay, who will not have made that preparation before hand, for which they, when near their departure, will wish they had done: and probably they will raise their warning voice, entreating others not to be so foolish as they have been; which warning will, no doubt soon be forgotten by the heedless and unreflecting.

We have no doubt, but what wickedness will continue to increase in the land; and the times grow more and more perilous; for Paul has given us to understand, "that in the last days perilous times shall come," and then he gives his reasons why they will be so. 2nd. Tim. III, 5 first verses.

And if we have not arrived at the verge of the last days, we think from the signs of the times, that we are very fast progressing towards them: and yet, notwithstanding the clearness which the sacred writers have pointed them out; we have every reason to fear that they will roll on unawares, and unperceived by the great mass of the people as did the flood in the days of Noah, until they will call to the rocks, and the mountains, to fall upon them, and hide them from the face of him who sitteth upon the throne; and from the wrath of the Lamb; for the great day of his wrath is come, and who shall be able to stand: Rev. VI, 16 and 17.

We feel to continue to warn our fellow travellers [travelers] to eternity generally, especially our brethren, to shun the paths of vice, and cleave to the rod of iron, which is the word of God; and pursue the path of righteousness, progressing in holiness from day to day, that we may become perfected in Christ Jesus, and prepared for every good word and work. Then let come what will, *prosperity* or *adversity*, *peace* or *persecution*, *liberty* or *bonds*, *life* or *death*, all will be well with us, for we shall have a conscience void of offence [offense], which will enable us to meet any or all of these things with composure, and resignation; and even with rejoicing, being buoyed up in every time of need, with the spirit of the living God; which will soothe our woes, soften our afflictions, and cause us to rejoice in the times of our greatest calamity and deepest distress.

We have received a copy of the history of the late persecution in Missouri, written by P. P. Pratt, while imprisoned in that State;

published at Detroit, Michigan. It contains 84 pages written in a concise and comprehensive manner; beginning with the outrages of Jackson county, he exhibits the most conspicuous characters' in their unhallowed conduct from that time, until the whole society of the saints were driven from the State. It contains an account of his miraculous escape from prison, also the escape of Elder Morris Phelps, at the same time. We could say much in favor of the style and boldness of the writer, but this is not our object; the plain unvarnished statement of facts, which can be demonstrated by thousands; is what pleases us, though it's but a small pamphlet, yet we would that *all* ears were made to hear it, and that every true Republican would awake from the slumber that has so long pervaded this Republic, and no longer suffer innocence to groan under the lash of murderers and tyrants. and would raise the standard of "equal rights." and bring to condign punishment, those that have trampled with impunity upon our wholsome [wholesome] constitution, and made laws and Justice a mere *by-word*.

In this No. will be seen an article which we copy from the New York Era." Signed P. P. Pratt, it's in contradiction to the foolish simple priest fabricated tale that has been going the rounds, charging Sidney Rigdon with the crime of making the Book of Mormon, out of the romantic writings of one Solomon Spaulding &c. We can mingle our testimony with that of Elder Pratt's, we concur in his statement; we can assure the public that from our own personal knowledge, Elder Pratt has given a plain statement of facts.

We also subjoin the copy of a letter written by one Mr. Haven from Mass. to his daughter in Quincy, Ill. which shows to a demonstration, that Mrs. Davidson did not write the letter, and that it was written, signed and circulated without her knowledge. Consequently it was got up by priests, and circulated by priests, upon her credit; the reason for getting it up, we think is obvious, for fair arguments, & every other means had failed to put down the truth, and this was the last resort; this having failed, we think that both priests and people will hereafter sit in silence upon this subject.

ERRATA

In our last No. on the 29th page, in the communication from the High council, it was dated Commerce, November 1839, which should have been stricken out entirely. Also an error at the bottom of the article, which escaped our notice, it is now dated 1830, but should be 1839.

In the Obituary, third paragraph, it reads thus: In this place, Nov. 2nd, Mahew Hillman. It should read November 22nd.

Detroit, Michigan, Oct. 12th 1839

EDITORS OF THE TIMES AND SEASONS

Dear Brethren.

We arrived here in 3 weeks, Distance 520 miles. Found it very sickly in every place, many taverns shut, and Bakery's closed on account of sickness; we are generally well, Br. Clark and O. Pratt started down the Lake two days ago, they were well. I have published a history of the persecution. A Pamphlet containing 84 pages. It came out of the Press Thursday last. The news papers, for the last three weeks have teemed with our sufferings and the outrages in Missouri. Every part of the country feels indignant at these unparallelled [unparalleled] outrages. You have doubtless heard of the Large meetings on the subject, in N. Y. and other places.-There are some 50 members of the church, within one day's journey of Detroit. Elder Savine, from N. Y. lives among them, great doors are opened for preaching, O. Pratt preached for some two weeks in Michigan, to crowded houses. Many believed, and some 22 dollars were given him for the journey. I preached once in the Detroit city hall. I just heard news from Elder Blakeslee, Jefferson co. N. Y., he baptized 100. *

* We started down the Lake to day, excuse my haste. I will write again soon.

Our love to all, inquiring friends. P. P. PRATT. -----

The following conference minutes, should have had a place in the December No. but, as we were sick when they came to hand, and several weeks behind our business, in consequence of our sickness, they were overlooked; but we think they are too interesting to pass them by, we therefore give them a place; likewise a short note from Elder Samuel James, disabusing the public in relation to a false report that has been going the rounds; with a short extract of a letter from the same sheet, we think it all interesting.-Ed.

CONFERENCE MINUTES.

August 9th A. D. 1839.

Agreeably to appointment a number of the official, and private members of the church of Latter day Saints; met in conference, at the house of Br. Caleb Bennets, Monmouth county New Jersey.

The meeting was called to order, by Br. Benj. Winchester, and Br. John P. Green was nominated, and elected President, and Samuel James Clerk. The meeting was then opened by singing and prayer by brother Greene.

High Priests present, John P. Green, Samuel James.

Seventy's , Jonathan Dumham, Benj. Winchester, Alexander Wright.

Elders, Joseph T. Ball, Josiah Ells.

Eleven members.

The conference was addressed by Br. Greene, in a feeling manner, concerning the object of the meeting, and the priveledge [privilege] of the members.

Then Br. Greene's letter of recommendation, from the Presidency of the church, requesting aid, in behalf of our aflicted [afflicted] brethren in the West, was read; and the following resolution adopted, that we will assist them, according to their ability; and recommend the same to our brethren.

Br. Winchester addressed the meeting on the subject of ordination; and Br. Greene read, in the Book of Covenants, the duties of the several officers of the church; and impressed the subject, by appropriate observations.

The subject was then discussed by several.

It was moved, seconded, and carried by vote, that Lewis James, be ordained a priest.

Brother Winchester gave an interesting account of his labours [labors], manner of teaching, the last year; & represented the branch of Monmouth co. N. J. of fifty members, in good standing.

Brother Greene addressed the meeting on the subject of teaching; and represented the branches, in the city of New York, and Brooklin in good fellowship.

Brother Ball represented the branches, Shrewsbury N. J. of twenty members. Montage three. Minissink N. H. two. Albany eight, Holliston Mass. sixteen in good fellowship.

Brother Dunham represented the branch in Hamilton, Madison co. N. H. of forty six in good fellowship.

Samuel James represented the branch in Leechburgh, Pa. of forty in good fellowship.

The meeting then closed by prayer.

On Saturday, br. Dunham and br. Greene, addressed an attentive congregation.

The work is prospering, and spreading, in this country. We have appointed a woods meeting on the 28th, at which, we expect the twelve; and anticipate much good.

JOHN P. GREENE, pres't.

Samuel James, Clerk.

Dear Brother, While there is room, I would give you some information of myself, and the prosperity of the cause in this region: I, in company with my brother came here the last of June, and have been here, and in the city of New York ever since, we left home the 15th of May, and visited several churches in Pa., who are generally strong in the faith; there is one church at Leechburgh, 40 miles east of Pittsburgh, on the canal, that was raised last winter by Father Nickerson of 41 members. Brother Barnes is in Chester county Pa. 30 miles from Philadelphia, and has baptized (the last account) 30, and the work prospering.

Since I came here I have baptized 6, and B. Winchester 2, and next Thursday I will baptize several more there is a great work through this country, and a prospect of many embracing the truth, the persecution has had a tendency to elicit inquiry, rather than surpress [suppress] the truth; the Priests have been rather troublesome, but their great effort has been, and still is, to keep the people from hearing, but they cannot prevail, they will hear and some embrace the truth. SAMUEL JAMES.

D. C. SMITH.

D. C. Smith, Dear brother, in the new covenant.

I request the following note to be inserted in the Times and Seasons, that the Brethren, and public may know the truth.

That whereas, a report has gone forth, that I (on a visit to the west last fall, during the persecution) joined the enemies, and did not make myself known to the brethren. I have only to say that the report is utterly false. SAMUEL JAMES.

THE MORMONITES.

To the Editor of the New Era: Sir: In your paper of the 25th inst. there is an article copied from the Boston Recorder, Headed "Mormon Bible," and signed "Matilda Davidson," which, justice to our society and to the public requires me to answer and I trust that a sense of justice will induce you sir, to give your readers both sides of the question.

I am one of the society who believe the "Book of Mormon," and as such I am assailed in the statement professing to come from Matilda Davidson.

In the first place there is no such book in existence as the "Mormon Bible." The Mormons, as they are vulgarly called, believe in the same Bible that all Cristendom professes to believe in, viz: the common version of the Old and New Testament. The Book of Mormon is not entitled a Bible, except by those who misrepresent it. It is entitled the "Book of Mormon."

The religious sect alluded to in your paper, are there accused of knavery and superstition. Now we are not sensible of being guilty of knavery, and we do not know wherein we are superstitious, but very much desire to know, in order that we may reform. If some good minister or editor will condescend to particulars, and point out our superstitions we will take it as a great kindness, for we are the declared enemies to knavery and superstition.

If a firm belief in the Gospel of a crusified [crucified] and risen Redeemer, as manifested to all nations, and as recorded in their sacred books, amount to superstition, than we are superstitious. If preaching that system to others and calling them to repentance, is superstition, then we are superstitious. If refusing to fellowship the modern systems of sectarianism which are contrary to the pure doctrines of the Bible, be superstition, then we are superstitious, for we hereby declare our withdrawal from all the mysticism, priestcraft and superstitions, and from all the creeds, doctrines, commandments, traditions and precepts of men, as far as they are contrary to the ancient faith and doctrine of the Saints; and we hereby bear our testimony against them.

We do not believe that God ever instituted more than one religious system under the same dispensation, therefore we do not admit that two different sects can possibly be right.-The churches of Jesus Christ, in any age or country, must be all built upon the same faith, the same baptism, the same Lord, the same holy spirit, which would guide them in all truth, and consequently from all error and superstition. The Book of Mormon has never been placed by us in the place of the sacred scriptures stand in their own place, and the Book of Mormon abundantly corroborates and bears testimony of the truth of the bible.-Indeed there is no society, within our knowledge, whose members adhere more closely to the Bible than ours.-For proof of this we appeal to the multitudes who attend our religious meetings in this city and in all other places.

The piece in your paper states that "Sidney Rigdon was connected in the printing office of Mr. Patterson," (in Pittsburg) and that "this is a fact well known in that region," and as Rigdon himself has frequently stated. Here he had ample opportunity to become acquainted with Mr. Spaulding's manuscript (Romance) and to copy it if he chose." This statement is utterly and entirely false. Mr. Rigdon was never connected with the said printing establishment, either directly, or indirectly, and we defy the world to bring proof of any such connection. Now the person or persons who fabricated that falsehood would do well to repent, and become persons of truth and veracity before they express such acute sensibility concerning the religious pretensions of others. The statement that Mr. Rigdon is one of the founders of the said religious sect is also incorrect.

The sect was founded in the state of New York while Mr. Rigdon resided on Ohio, several hundred miles distant. Mr. Rigdon embraced the doctrine through my instrumentality. I first presented the Book of Mormon to him. I stood upon the bank of the stream while he was baptized, and assisted to officiate in his ordination, and I myself was unacquainted with the system until some months after its organization, which was on the sixth of April, 1830, and I embraced it in September following.

The piece further states that "a woman preacher appointed a meeting at New Salem, Ohio, and in the meeting read and repeated copious extracts from the Book of Mormon. Now it is a fact well known, that we have not had a female preacher in our connection, for we do not believe in a female priesthood. It further says that the excitement in New Salem became so great that the inhabitants had a meeting and deputed Doctor Philastus Hurlburt, one of their members, to repair to Spaulding's widow, and obtain from her the original manuscript of the romance, &c. But the statement does not say whether he obtained the manuscript, but still leaves the impression that he did, and that it was compared with the Book of Mormon. Now whoever will read the work got up by said Hurlburt entitled "Mormonism Unveiled," will find that he there states that the said manuscript of Spaulding's romance was lost and could no where be found. But the widow is here made to say that it is carefully preserved. Here seems to be some knavery or crooked work; and no wonder, for this said Hurlburt is one of the most notorious rascals in the western country. He was first cut off from our society for an attempt at seduction and crime, and secondly he was laid under bonds in Geauga county, Ohio, for threatening to murder Joseph Smith, Jr., after which he laid a deep design of the Spaulding romance imposition, in which he has been backed by evil and designing men in different parts of the country, and sometimes by those who do not wish to do wrong, but who are ignorant on the subject. Now what but falsehood could be expected from such a person?-Now if there is such a manuscript in existence, let it come forward at once, and not be kept in the dark. Again, if the public will be patient, they will doubtless find that the piece singed "Matilda Davidson" (Spaulding's widow) is a base fabrication by Priest Storrs of Holliston, Mass., in order to save his craft, after losing the deacon of his church, and several of its most pious and intelligent members, who left his society to embrace what they considered to be truth. At any rate, a judge of literary productions, who can swallow that piece of writing as the production of a woman in private life, can be made to believe that the Book of Mormon is a romance. For the one is as much like a romance as the other is like a woman's composition.

The production, signed Matilda Davidson, is evidently the work of a man accustomed to public address, and the Book of Mormon I know to be true, and the Spaulding story, as far as the origin of the Book of Mormon is connected with it, I know to be false.

I now leave the subject with a candid public, with a sincere desire, that those who have been deluded with such vain and foolish lies, may be undeceived.

Editors, who have given publicity to the Spaulding story, will do an act of justice by giving publicity to the foregoing.

P. P. PRATT .N. Y. Nov. 27, 1839

[From the Quincy Whig]

A CUNNING DEVICE DETECTED. It will be recollected that a few months since an article appeared in several of the papers, purporting to give an account of the origin of the Book of Mormon. How far the writer of that piece has effected his purposes, or what his purposes were in pursuing the course he has, I shall not attempt to say at this time, but shall call upon every candid man to judge in this matter for himself, and shall content myself by presenting before the public the other side of the question in the form of a letter, as follows:

Copy of a letter written by Mr. John Haven of Holliston, Middlesex co. Massachusetts, to his daughter Elizabeth Haven of Quincy, Adams co., Illinois.

Your brother Jesse passed through Monson where he saw Mrs. Davidson and her daughter, Mrs. McKinistry, and also Dr. Ely and spent several hours with them, during which time he asked them the following questions, viz:

Did you, Mrs. Davidson, write a letter to John Storrs, giving an account of the origin of the Book of Mormon? Ans: I did not. Did you sign your name to it? Ans: I did not, neither did I ever see the letter until I saw it in the Boston Recorder, the letter was never brought to me to sign. Ques. What agency had you in having this letter sent to Mr. Storrs? Ans: D. R. Austin came to my house and asked me some questions, took some minutes on paper, and from these minutes wrote that letter. Question. Is what is written in the letter true? Ans: In the main it is.-Ques. Have you read the book of

Mormon? Ans. I have read some in it; Ques. Does Mr. Spauldings manuscript, and the Book of Mormon agree? I think some few of the names are alike.-Ques. Does the manuscript describe an idolatrous or a religious people? Ans. An Idolatrous people. Ques. Where is the manuscript. Ans: Dr. P. Hurlburt came here and took it, said he would get it printed, and let me have one-half the profits. Ques. Has Dr. P. Hurlburt got the manuscript printed? Ans: I received a letter stating it did not read as they expected, and they should not print it. Ques. How large is Mr. Spaulding's manuscript? Ans: about one third as large as the Book of Mormon. Ques. To Mrs. McKenestry, how old was you when your father wrote the manuscript? Ans: About five years of age. Ques. Did you ever read the manuscript? Ans: When I was about twelve years old, I used to read it for diversion. Ques. Did the manuscript describe an Idolatrous or a religious people. Ans. An Idolatrous people. Ques.- Does the manuscript and the Book of Mormon agree? Ans: I think some of the names agree. Ques. Are you certain that some of the names agree? Ans: I am not. Ques. Have you ever read any in the Book of Mormon? Ans: I have not. Ques. Was your name attached to that letter which was sent to Mr. John Storrs by your order? Ans: No, I never meant that my name should be there.

You see by the above questions and answers, that Mr. Austin, in his great zeal, to destroy the Latter Day Saints, has asked Mrs. Davidson a few questions, then wrote a letter to Mr. Storrs, in his own language. I do not say that the above questions and answers, were given in the form that I have written them, but these questions were asked, and these answers given. Mrs. Davidson is about seventy years of age, and somewhat broke. This may certify that I am personally acquainted with Mr. Havens, his son and daughter, and am satisfied they are person of truth. I have also read Mr. Haven's letter to his Daughter, which has induced me to copy it for publication, and I further say, the above is a correct copy of Mr. Havens letter. A. BADLAM.

The West Chester Village Record says the Mormons are holding a protracted meeting at the Nantmeal seminary, in this county. We understand that about forty members have been baptized in all.-N. Y. Era.

NOTICE

It is proper to say that at our conference October inst. that a species of accusation appeared against Elder Harlow Redfield, insomuch [inasmuch] that he was suspended and required to answer to the High Council at this place. In compliance therewith, he this day appeared when no charge came against him, nor was it found proper that any should come. Therefore the council restored to him full; fellowship, and all official standing the same as if not such suspension had taken place. H. G. SHERWOOD, Clerk.

Nauvoo, Oct. 20, 1839.

****

PRATT'S DEFENCE. [DEFENSE]

As down a lone dungeon, with darkness o'er-spread The mob soon dispersed, to the Rulers appealed,

In silence and sorrow I made my lone bed, Saying, lend us your aid, and the Mormons will yield,

While for from my prison my friends had retired. For surely they never were known to resist

And joy from this bosom had almost expired. A mob when commissioned by rulers and priests.

From all that was lovely, constrained for to part, This soon was considered by far the best plan;

From wife and from children so dear to my heart; And orders were issued for ten thousand men;

While foes were exulting, and friends far away, Including the Wilson's and Gillum's of course,

In half broken slumbers, all pensive I lay. And all the mob forces, for better, for worse.

I thought upon Zion-her sorrowful doom:- These soon were forthcoming, in dreadful array;

I thought on her anguish-her trouble and gloom, Some painted like Indians, all armed for the fray;

How for years she had wandered, a captive forlorn, The Mormons soon yielded without the first fire,

Cast out and afflicted, and treated with scorn. And the mobers accomplished their utmost desire.

I thought on the time when some five years ago, Some females were ravished-and cattle and grain

Twelve hundred from Jackson, were driven by foes, Became a free booty-and one pris'ner slain.

While two hundred houses to ashes were burned:- Some twenty or thirty were murderd [murdered] outright,

Our flourishing fields to a desert were turned. And ten thousand others were BANISHED THE STATE:

I remembered these crimes still unpunished remained, By what LAW of the Statute to me is unknown;

And the life oft repeated-again, and again, But it must be by law all these great things were done,

From counties adjoining, cempelled [compelled] to remove. For the next Legislature the expense to defray,

We purchased in Caldwell, prairie and grove. Voted two hundred thousand, the soldiers to pay.

And there 'mid the wild flowers, that bloomed o'er the plain: To resist THIS oppression-THESE excellent laws,

Our rights and our freedom, we thought to maintain: Was murder; and treason; (in technical clause.)

Nor dreamed that oppression would drive us from thence, While women and children were driven away,

The laws of our country we claimed for defence. [defense] Their husbands and fathers in prison must stay.

But soon as kind autumn rewarded our toil So now to the Jury and Judge I submit;

And plenty around us began for to smile, I'm not learned in such laws.-they may hang or aquit [acquit]-

Our foes were assembled-being tempted with gain: But though they; should hang me, or keep me in jail,

To ravage and plunder, and drive us again. The spirit of Freedom and Truth will prevail.

When many were driven, and plunderd [plundered] and rob'd,

And some had been murdrd [murdered] by this dreadful mob,-

When cries for redress and protection were

We arose in our strength, our own rights to maintain.

OBITUARY.

DIED-In this place, on the 10th Inst. Stephen Shumway, in the 34th year of his age.--In this place, on the 1st Inst. Moroni, Son of John D. and Hariet Parker, aged 4 years 3 months and 4 days.

THE TIMES AND SEASONS,

Is printed and published every month, at Commerce, Hancock co. Ill. by E. ROBINSON AND D. C. SMITH, EDITORS AND PROPRIETORS.

TERMS. ONE DOLLAR per annum, payable, in all cases, in advance. Any person procuring 10 subscribers, and forwarding us ten dollars current money, shall receive one volume gratis.

www.ingramcontent.com/pod-product-compliance
Lightning Source LLC
LaVergne TN
LVHW041633070426
835507LV00008B/594